D1348363

The
NEWCASTLE
MISCELLANY

The
NEWCASTLE
MISCELLANY

By MIKE 'BIFFA' BOLAM

VSP

Vision Sports Publishing
19–23 High Street
Kingston on Thames
Surrey
KT1 1LL

www.visionsp.co.uk

Published by Vision Sports Publishing in 2012

Text © Mike Bolam
Cover illustrations © Steve Gulbis
Inside illustrations © Bob Bond Sporting Caricatures
Additional illustrations © Hutch

ISBN 13: 978-1-907637-74-2

All rights reserved. No part of this publication may be reproduced,
stored in a retrieval system, or transmitted in any form or by any
means, electronic, mechanical, photocopying, recording or otherwise,
without the prior permission of the publishers.

This book is sold subject to the condition that it shall not, by way
of trade or otherwise, be lent, re-sold, hired out, or otherwise
circulated without the publisher's prior consent in any form of
binding or cover other than that in which it is published and without
a similar condition including this condition being imposed on the
subsequent purchaser.

Printed and bound in China by Toppan Printing Co Ltd

Typeset in Sabon MT by Palimpsest Book Production Limited,
Falkirk, Stirlingshire

A CIP catalogue record for this book is
available from the British Library

Author's Acknowledgements

I would like to thank Paul Joannou and Alan Candlish for their encouragement and assistance in writing this book, as well as Jim Drewett and Clive Batty at Vision Sports Publishing for helping me produce it.

Credit is also due to my co-writer at NUFC.com, Niall Mackenzie and the readers of that website for their input and continued support.

Thanks also to Karen for her invaluable assistance and endless patience in putting up with the author on a daily basis.

To everyone else involved – you know who you are – Biffa says Cheers!

Mike 'Biffa' Bolam

Author's note: The term 'competitive match' is used throughout this book as describing Football League, Premiership, FA Cup, League Cup and European games only. Other competitions including Northern League, War Leagues, Anglo-Italian, Anglo-Scottish and Texaco Cups are not included unless stated.

All stats in *The Newcastle Miscellany* are correct up until the end of the 2011/12 season.

Foreword
By Rob Lee

Although I'd played and scored at St James' Park with Charlton Athletic, it was only after signing for Newcastle United in 1992 that I came to understand what football on Tyneside really meant.

The tale of how Kevin Keegan convinced me to turn down a move to Middlesbrough in favour of becoming a Magpie is well-known, although I never did think that Newcastle was closer to London! My family links with the North East actually go back decades and I have relatives who were on the Jarrow March.

In the end though, the influence of Kevin Keegan made me opt not to join my old boss Lennie Lawrence on Teesside. KK was – and is – a hero of mine, going back to when he starred for Liverpool, and playing under him was a revelation in terms of belief and confidence.

One of the first things Kevin said to me when I met him was that I could play for England. And although I dismissed that at the time as something he told every home-grown player, within two years he was to be proved right.

Scoring on my international debut against Romania in 1994 remains a treasured memory, as does lining up at Wembley against Nigeria alongside my Newcastle team-mates Peter Beardsley and Steve Howey – and some bloke called Shearer.

After sharing with John Beresford on away trips with United, I then roomed with Alan and we became great mates – a friendship that has survived, despite my breaking his nose!

I have to add that it was a total accident and came after I'd joined Derby County and he was still at Newcastle. We both went for the same ball and clashed heads, needing stitches in head wounds. What made it worse for him though was that he'd had a similar whack earlier that season from another former colleague, Manchester City's Steve Howey!

To be playing against a club you'd been with for a decade was a strange feeling, but the reception from the Newcastle fans that day was first class. In fairness though, that was no surprise after having seen the reception that former team-mates such as Gavin Peacock and David Kelly had received.

Both Gav and 'Ned' were in the Newcastle side on that incredible day that we beat Leicester City 7–1 to seal promotion. And after hitting the ground running back in the top flight, to mark the club's return to European competition with a hat trick of headers against Antwerp was another personal high point.

Not all of my memories of life at United are as pleasant though, and I probably have Kevin Phillips and Niall Quinn to thank for extending my time at the club. Had they not scored on that dreadful night in 1999 when Sunderland beat us, then Ruud Gullit would have stayed and both Alan and myself moved on.

When writing my autobiography in 2000, I paid tribute to Newcastle fans for their passion, knowledge and loyalty – little knowing that those qualities would be severely tested and that the Championship Trophy I'd lifted in 1993 would once again be paraded around Gallowgate in 2010.

By the way, the decision not to emulate the 1993 side and mark promotion with an open top bus tour round the city was the correct one, as like many fans I felt the club should have been relegated and regaining our rightful place wasn't cause for proper celebration. The scenes in the Bigg Market were probably much the same though!

Whenever I meet Toon fans, the subject that always comes up is the 1995/96 season, when we were pipped to the Premier League title by Manchester United. It remains a massive regret that we couldn't pull it off, but the momentum that Alex Ferguson's side built up became unstoppable.

We played them off the park at Gallowgate, but Peter Schmeichel was unbelievable in goal, and you never saw Eric Cantona all game until he scored with probably his only kick. Looking back, that was probably the turning point - even if we had drawn that game I think we would have gone on to win the title.

Happily, there have been great days in the history of this great club and many of them are detailed here. Lifelong black and whiters like Steve Harper have had the exploits of Jackie Milburn drummed into them from an early age, but for honorary Geordies like myself, this is a handy way to catch up.

Dipping into this book, I'm also reminded of stars like Bryan 'Pop' Robson, who was in the West Ham team when I was first taken to Upton Park by my granddad in the early 1970s. It's no secret that the Hammers were my team and playing a handful of games for them late in my career was a highlight, as was seeing my sons Oliver and Elliot both sign for the club.

While Oliver was born in London shortly before my family moved to the North East, Elliot arrived during my time in Toon, when we were living in Durham. And I was present in 2011 to see him achieve something I never did – a goal against the Mackems. Not content with one though, he went on to claim a hat trick against the red and whites in an Academy match.

Scoring in an FA Cup semi-final was the closest I got to winning proper silverware with Newcastle; I only hope that I'm present when they eventually collect that longed-for and elusive trophy. It'll be some party.

Rob Lee
June 2012

— FROM EASTENDERS TO WEST END BOYS —

Football was first played at St James' Park in October 1880, with a team called Newcastle Rangers occupying the site – although they were to play no part in the creation of the side that went on to be named Newcastle United.

In November 1881, a team named Stanley were founded by the cricket club of the same name, playing on a pitch at Stanley Street, Byker. Eleven months later Stanley changed their name to Newcastle East End and incorporated another recently-founded local team, Rosewood. By 1886 East End were on the move again, this time further out into the Eastern suburbs of Newcastle on Chillingham Road.

Elsewhere in the city, meanwhile, August 1882 had seen the formation of another football club, Newcastle West End, by the cricket club of the same name, playing initially on the Town Moor before relocating near to the Great North Road in Jesmond three years later. Then in May 1886 West End acquired the lease of St James Park, which hadn't been regularly used since Rangers moved out to a site in Byker in 1882.

West End and East End were by now the biggest clubs on Tyneside and, having regularly faced each other in friendlies since their inception and in the Northern League from season 1889/90, became arch rivals. However it was East End who came to dominate both in footballing and financial terms, winning 2–0 and 3–0 at St James' Park in the league and FA Cup respectively in October 1891 and the return game 7–1 at their Heaton Junction ground the following February.

Within three months of that crushing derby defeat West End were declared insolvent. However, rather than lose St James' Park to football, they sportingly offered the lease to their biggest rivals. East End gratefully took them up, kicking off life at St James' Park with a friendly against Celtic in September 1892 watched by 6,000 supporters. Then on December 9th, a public meeting was held seeking agreement on a new name in a bid to increase interest amongst the Tyneside public, with Newcastle United being decided upon.

The rest is history . . . with Newcastle United accepting an invitation to join the Football League (one that East End had rejected the previous season) along with fellow new boys Liverpool, Woolwich Arsenal, Rotherham Town and Middlesbrough Ironopolis in Division Two for the 1893/94 campaign.

— CHAMPIONS! —

Newcastle United: Champions!

The fourth and most recent occasion on which Newcastle United were crowned top-flight champions came on Saturday April 23rd 1927, a 1–1 draw at West Ham United confirming title success with two games still to play.

Only 21 players were used by the Magpies all season, with goalkeeper Willie Wilson, left-back Frank Hudspeth and outside-left Stan Seymour appearing in all 42 games. Top scorer with 36 strikes from 38 appearances was Hughie Gallacher, the talented but temperamental Scottish striker who had controversially succeeded Hudspeth as club captain that season. Seasonal highlights included a 4–0 opening day success over Aston Villa on Tyneside, with Gallacher grabbing all the goals.

United hit top spot for the first time in mid-January after completing the double over Villa. The Magpies' nearest challengers Huddersfield were then beaten 1–0 at St James' Park on Good Friday, 24 hours before Spurs were dispatched 3–2 at the same venue.

Newcastle did take possession of the Football League Trophy again in both 1993 and 2010, Barry Venison collecting it the first time before Nicky Butt and Alan Smith did the honours seven years later. By that point, however, the accolade was to recognise title success in the second tier of English Football.

Divison One Table, 1926/27:

	P	W	D	L	F	A	Pts
Newcastle United	42	25	6	11	96	58	56
Huddersfield Town	42	17	17	8	76	60	51
Sunderland	42	21	7	14	98	70	49
Bolton Wanderers	42	19	10	13	84	62	48
Burnley	42	19	9	14	91	80	47
West Ham United	42	19	8	15	86	70	46
Leicester City	42	17	12	13	85	70	46
Sheffield United	42	17	10	15	74	86	44
Liverpool	42	18	7	17	69	61	43
Aston Villa	42	18	7	17	81	83	43
The Arsenal	42	17	9	16	77	86	43
Derby County	42	17	7	18	86	73	41
Tottenham Hotspur	42	16	9	17	76	78	41
Cardiff City	42	16	9	17	55	65	41
Manchester United	42	13	14	15	52	64	40
The Wednesday	42	15	9	18	75	92	39
Birmingham	42	17	4	21	64	73	38
Blackburn Rovers	42	15	8	19	77	96	38
Bury	42	12	12	18	68	77	36
Everton	42	12	10	20	64	90	34
Leeds United	42	11	8	23	69	88	30
West Bromwich Albion	42	11	8	23	65	86	30

— THEY CALL US NEWCASTLE UNITED —

"People are very proud of Newcastle, very proud to come from here. This is a working class City and they just want to enjoy themselves and live life to the full. "They work all week, pick their wages up at the end of the week and they spend it over a weekend by having a good time and watching the football. That's our life."
Alan Shearer

"The club wasn't the best-run club. It was a disaster in many ways, but the supporters made up for it."
Tony Green

"The reaction of the fans is amazing. To have 50,000 people singing a song about me is unbelievable. I'm not from this country and my family are in Argentina, but I feel the love of the fans."
Fabricio Coloccini

"When you ran out at St James' Park, the hairs on the back of your neck stood up. Wembley didn't do anything for me."
Charlie Crowe

"When I speak about my career, the time at Newcastle was the best five years of my life. It was as if I was at home. At first, I couldn't understand what the fans were saying, and I would have to just nod and smile, but after a while it was fine."
Philippe Albert

"I absolutely loved playing at Newcastle as the fans made it a very special club. There is a misconception that they don't like Londoners – that's not true. You can be from London, Manchester, Liverpool or wherever. As long as you give 100 per cent every time you play, they will appreciate you. If you have a bit of ability on top of that, they will take you to their hearts."
Paul Goddard

"For local passion for a team, I don't think that there is anywhere that can beat Newcastle."
Dave Hilley

"Playing at Newcastle is one of the best places to play for any player – you are so well backed and what you give on the pitch comes back to you from the stands. The Geordie fans really look after you in that sense and you can use it to help you achieve results. It's a real passion up in Newcastle and the lifestyle is very much about the team."
David Kelly

— STADIUM OF DELIGHT —

Having drawn four and won the other two of their final visits to Roker Park, Newcastle have found the red and white's replacement Stadium of Light at nearby Wearmouth equally to their liking, with just one defeat in their nine visits by the end of the 2011/12 season as follows:

1999/00	drew 2–2 (2–1)	Didier Domi, Helder
2000/01	drew 1–1 (0–0)	Andy O'Brien
2001/02	won 1–0 (0–0)	Nicos Dabizas
2002/03	won 1–0 (1–0)	Nobby Solano (pen)
2005/06	won 4–1 (0–1)	Michael Chopra, Alan

		Shearer (pen), Charles
		N'Zogbia, Albert Luque
2007/08	drew 1–1 (0–0)	James Milner
2008/09	lost 1–2 (1–1)	Shola Ameobi
2010/11	drew 1–1 (0–0)	Kevin Nolan
2011/12	won 1–0 (0–0)	Ryan Taylor

The goals scored by Helder, O'Brien, Chopra, Luque and Taylor were their first for United in the Premier League – while Alan Shearer's was his 148th and last for the club, sustaining a career-ending injury and leaving the field ten minutes after scoring.

— ALL TIME PREMIER LEAGUE TABLE —

A 3–1 success away at West Bromwich Albion in March 2012 saw Newcastle join an exclusive set of clubs to have broken through the 1,000 point mark in the Premier League. And the 500-point barrier had also been reached on the road, as a result of a 4–0 victory away to Bolton Wanderers in October 2001.

Team	P	W	D	L	F	A	Pts
Manchester United	772	500	163	109	1541	660	1663
Arsenal	772	415	204	153	1345	717	1449
Chelsea	772	401	199	172	1282	741	1402
Liverpool	772	380	194	198	1236	753	1334
Aston Villa	772	283	240	249	973	923	1089
Tottenham Hotspur	772	294	204	274	1072	1020	1086
Everton	772	272	218	282	974	979	1034
Newcastle United	692	277	186	229	996	885	1017

In terms of points gained, the Magpies sit eighth in the rankings of the 45 clubs to have competed in the Premier League.

— NEWCASTLE LEGENDS: JACKIE MILBURN —

Wor Jackie

Commemorated in books, plays, statues and songs, 'Wor Jackie' enjoyed a lifelong association with Newcastle United and his legend lives on two decades after his death.

Born into a footballing family (which included second cousins Jack and Bobby Charlton), Milburn's reputation was forged in the black and white of Newcastle and, for many football fans, he came to symbolise the club like no other player before or since.

Milburn's Magpies association began in 1943 when, as a 19 year-old, he played two trial matches at St James' Park – scoring twice in the first then blasting home six second-half goals the following weekend. This demonstration of powerful and accurate shooting was a taste of things to come.

His home debut in a war-time match in August 1943 was marked with a goal scored with his first touch, but Milburn had to wait until an end to hostilities and the start of the 1945/46 season to make his competitive bow.

A season before Football League fixtures returned, his debut came in the FA Cup, staged that season over two legs to assist clubs financially. Two goals in a 4–2 win over Barnsley sent a 60,284 crowd away from Gallowgate happy – although a 0–3 second leg reverse at Oakwell ended any Wembley dreams.

Then manager George Martin was to have a profound effect on Milburn's career in 1947, moving him to centre forward from the wing and handing him the number nine shirt. The switch paid instant dividends with a hat-trick away at Bury and a haul of 20 league goals that season as the Magpies returned to Division One.

However, it's for Milburn's FA Cup final exploits that he is best remembered: netting twice against Blackpool in the 1951 final and scoring after 45 seconds against Manchester City in 1955 en route to collecting a third winner's medal.

Many contemporary observers choose the sixth round tie away at Portsmouth in March 1952 as his finest display, a game which featured a hat-trick of memorable strikes.

After having left Tyneside for Belfast club Linfield in 1957, Milburn returned to England three years later at the age of 36, and was greeted with a number of offers.

Amid interest from Stoke City and various Scottish sides came a call from Charlie Mitten – the then Newcastle boss. However, Milburn was denied the chance of a Toon comeback after the Football League refused to sanction a request to repay his player's insurance policy.

Turning down the job of Ashington player-manager, he took a similar position at Yiewsley in Middlesex and briefly, at Carmel College in Wallingford. Milburn then managed Ipswich Town but, after just 18 months in charge, returned to the north-east in 1962 to spend the next two decades reporting on Newcastle United for a Sunday newspaper.

A testimonial game followed in 1967, in front of over 45,000 fans, while 1981 saw him the unwitting subject of the popular TV show *This is Your Life*.

Sadly, lung cancer claimed Jackie Milburn in October 1988. His funeral cortege fittingly slowed on Barrack Road, opposite St James' Park, en route to St Nicholas' Cathedral amid unprecedented numbers of mourners. Milburn's widow Laura later scattered his ashes across the Gallowgate End of the ground before returning to christen the stand that now bears his name.

Jackie Milburn factfile
Born: Ashington, May 11th 1924 Died: October 9th 1988
Newcastle career: 397 apps, 200 goals (1943–57)
Other clubs: Linfield
International: England, 13 caps, 10 goals

— WHO THE **** ARE YOU? —

Sides that Newcastle United have never faced competitively:

Aldershot Town, Barnet, Burton Albion, Crawley Town, Dagenham
& Redbridge, Macclesfield Town, Milton Keynes Dons, Morecambe,
Rochdale*, Wycombe Wanderers, Yeovil Town.

* faced in wartime football

— MEMORY MATCHES 1 —

September 22nd

1984 QPR 5 Newcastle United 5 (Division One)

After embarking upon his first season as Newcastle manager with three
victories, Jack Charlton took his side to Shepherds Bush looking for
an improvement from a side that had subsequently slipped to a
worrying trio of defeats. Despite, playing on the unloved Loftus Road
plastic pitch, United raced into a third-minute lead when Chris Waddle
centred from the left for Neil Macdonald to head home from close in.
That woke up the home side and Newcastle had to defend in depth
before breaking away on 17 minutes and seeing Waddle round R's
'keeper Peter Hucker before finding the net. Midway through the half
it was 3–0, when Kenny Wharton's deflected volley rebounded off a
post and Waddle swept home the loose ball. And with England boss
Bobby Robson watching from the stands, Waddle completed his hat
trick four minutes before half time with a left-foot raker.

A chastened Rangers side returned to the fray after an ear-bashing
from manager Alan Mullery and with Ian Stewart on the field – a
second future Magpie winger, with Wayne Fereday already in situ.

Within five minutes Gary Bannister beat Kevin Carr at the second
attempt, and when United defender Peter Haddock somehow managed
to ricochet a clearance off Kenny Wharton and into his own net, the
black and whites went into meltdown.

The referee then spared Glenn Roeder's blushes by ruling out a Simon Stainrod effort after the Newcastle defender botched his clearance, but John Gregory's run found Carr in no-man's land and it became 4–3 on 74 minutes. At that point the home side seemed to lose their impetus and Newcastle's hopes of hanging on looked markedly better; increasing vastly when Waddle set up Wharton to score with just six minutes to play.

Unfortunately that sparked the Hoops back into life and Steve Wicks promptly headed home before Stewart played in Gary Micklewhite and he outpaced the visiting defence before swiping the ball home to make it 5–5 in the final seconds.

An incandescent Charlton called his side's performance,"a total embarrassment, absolutely diabolical…there are so many things wrong at Newcastle it is incredible."

NUFC: Carr, Brown, Saunders, McCreery, Anderson, Roeder, Haddock, Beardsley, Waddle, McDonald, Wharton.

— JUNIOR JACK —

Since 1998, Sport Newcastle (formerly the Newcastle Sports Council) have presented an award at their annual dinner to a rising star of the Newcastle United Academy.

The "Wor Jackie Trophy" is a miniature replica of the statue sculpted by Susanna Robinson and erected in Newcastle city centre. An appeal to raise the necessary funds was supported by the local *Evening Chronicle* newspaper, with their editor Graeme Stanton donating the replica to be used as a trophy.

His successors have continued to make the presentation, which has been collected by teenage Magpies born both in the North East and far further afield as follows:

Year	Winner and birthplace
1998	Aaron Hughes (Northern Ireland)
1999	Michael Chopra (Tyne and Wear)
2000	Gary Caldwell (Scotland)
2001	Shola Ameobi (Nigeria)
2002	Steven Taylor (London)
2003	Peter Ramage (Northumberland)
2004	Martin Brittain (Northumberland)
2005	Paul Huntington (Cumbria)
2006	Matty Pattison (South Africa)

2007	Andy Carroll (Tyne and Wear)
2008	Kazenga LuaLua (DR Congo)
2009	Nile Ranger (London)
2010	Brad Inman (Australia)
2011	Jak Alnwick (Northumberland)
2012	Remie Streete (Buckinghamshire)

— ST JAMES' PARK INTERNATIONALS —

Despite being initially selected as a venue for the 1966 World Cup Finals, wrangles over ground ownership and redevelopment between the club and Newcastle City Council saw the Football Association withdraw their hosting invitation in 1964. Middlesbrough's Ayresome Park was chosen to host three group stage ties instead, which were attended by the lowest crowds of the whole competition.

However, St James' Park has hosted various other senior international fixtures:

Date	Fixture	Competition
March 18th 1901	England 6 Wales 0	Home International
April 6th 1907	England 1 Scotland 1	Home International
November 15th 1933	England 1 Wales 2	Home International
November 9th 1938	England 4 Norway 0	Home International
June 10th 1996	Romania 0 France 1	Euro Championship
June 15th 1996	Bulgaria 1 Romania 0	Euro Championship
June 18th 1996	France 3 Bulgaria 1	Euro Championship
September 5th 2001	England 2 Albania 0	World Cup Qualifier
August 18th 2004	England 3 Ukraine 0	Friendly International
March 30th 2005	England 2 Azerbaijan 0	World Cup Qualifier
February 22nd 1950	England B 1 Holland B 0	B Friendly International
November 2nd 1960	England U23 1 Italy U23 1	U23 Friendly International
February 5th 1964	England U23 3 Scotland U23 2U23	Friendly International
March 1st 1967	England U23 1 Scotland U23 3U23	Friendly International
March 13th 1974	England U23 2 Scotland U23 0U23	Friendly International
April 26th 1983	England U21 1	Euro Championship

	Hungary U21 0U21	
November 15th 1994	England U21 1	Friendly International
	Eire U21 0 U21	
April 1st 2003	England U21 1	Friendly International
	Turkey U21 1U21	

St.James' Park was also selected as one of six UK venues for the 2012 Olympics; hosting a total of six fixtures in the Men's competition and three in the Women's.

The stadium has also been earmarked as one of six UK venues to host the football tournament at the 2012 Olympics.

— TYNE-TAMAR TRIBULATIONS —

The longest possible journey between English football league stadia remains the 820-mile round trip between Newcastle and Plymouth. To date there have been 37 competitive meetings between the two sides, with the Magpies having made 19 pilgrimages to Devon between 1905 and 2010.

And in addition to the long distance involved, the timing of those games has often caused headaches for the travelling contingent. However, United did benefit from one piece of fixture scheduling when a Second Division visit to Home Park was arranged for January 1963. The South West of England was less affected by the big freeze that decimated sports events that winter and Newcastle registered a 2–0 victory in what proved to be the only game they played between December 22nd 1962 and March 2nd 1963!

More recently, the December 1990 meeting of the sides was moved to a Sunday lunchtime kick-off in order for Argyle to benefit from using the stadium car park for a Christmas Shoppers Park and Ride Scheme. Another yuletide fiasco 12 months later for similar reasons then saw the game scheduled for the Friday evening before Christmas.

Faced with a return to Devon in the 2009/10 season following their demotion to the Championship, Newcastle supporters were then handed a second trip at short notice, when the FA Cup third round draw paired Argyle with United. Adverse weather conditions relented for long enough to allow the travelling Toon Army to journey by planes, trains and automobiles, but meteorological conditions would unexpectedly affect the Championship fixture at Home Park some three months later.

Fallout from volcanic eruptions in Iceland resulted in an ash cloud drifting into United Kingdom airspace and the grounding of many domestic flights. Already faced with a Monday night trek when the game was switched to a Monday evening for live TV transmission, some further re-jigging of travel plans was necessary – with the team travelling by coach. It didn't seem to affect them too much though, with a 2–0 victory confirming United's Championship title success and the long journey back to the North East allowing for more than a few celebratory drinks.

— BEFORE WE WERE SO RUDELY INTERRUPTED —

One immediate effect of Britain's formal declaration of war against Germany on September 3rd 1939 was the immediate suspension of competitive football fixtures. That meant that the opening games of the 1939/40 season were expunged from the records, including Newcastle's three games in Division Two:

Date	Result
August 26th 1939	Millwall 3 Newcastle United 0
August 30th 1939	Nottingham Forest 2 Newcastle United 0
September 2nd 1939	Newcastle United 8 Swansea Town 1

Lost to history therefore are the goals scored at St James' Park in an 8–1 win over Swansea Town on the last Saturday before war was declared – a hat-trick from Ray Bowden, two from Tommy Pearson and efforts from David Hamilton, Willie Scott and Billy Cairns.

When the Football League programme resumed after the war, the 1939/40 fixture list was resurrected, with United fairing rather better the second time round:

Date	Result
August 31st 1946	Millwall 1 Newcastle United 4
September 5th 1946	Nottingham Forest 0 Newcastle United 2
September 7th 1946	Newcastle United 1 Swansea Town 1

Appearing in both the opening game of 1939 and 1946 against Millwall at St James' Park were no fewer than five players: Tom Swinburne, Benny Craig, Duggie Wright, Jimmy Woodburn and Tommy Pearson. Of the other six Magpies who played in the 1939 Swansea Town game, five resumed their careers with various clubs after the end of hostilities. Bowden, however, never played competitive football again.

— KNOT FOR THE FAINT-HEARTED —

Gallows humour still thrives at St James' Park

Following a misguided attempt by the club to re-christen it as the South Stand, traditionalists were delighted in 2008 when the southern end of St. James' Park was again referred to as the Gallowgate Stand. That name dates from when the original standing terrace was built on the route from Newcastle's New Gate Gaol to the site of the town's gallows.

The last public execution at the gallows took place in 1844, less than 40 years before football was being played on the same site. On that occasion, a death sentence was served on Mark Sherwood of nearby Blandford Street for the murder of his wife.

Indeed Newcastle was synonymous for its big crowds long before a football was ever kicked at St James' Park. In 1829, more than 20,000 people turned up to witness the hanging of a notorious female murderer.

The exact site of the gallows is believed to have been adjacent to Leazes Terrace, on the site of what is now the East Stand.

— FAIRS CUP GLORY —

Famously, the last major trophy won by Newcastle United was the Fairs Cup of 1969. But exactly how Newcastle ended up in the competition that season is a story in itself.

The Inter Cities Fairs Cup was the precursor to the UEFA Cup, with the original 1955 rules admitting into the competition a single representative team for each city that organised trade fairs. That pretty soon fell by the wayside in favour of a one club per city entry policy.

When Newcastle ended the 1967/68 season in tenth place of Division One, this rule worked spectacularly in their favour. Champions Manchester City were joined in the European Cup by runners-up and holders Manchester United, third-placed Liverpool and fourth-placed Leeds United entering the Fairs Cup. The one-club, one-city rule excluded Everton in fifth spot, but admitted Chelsea in sixth as England's third Fairs Cup side, representing London. Tottenham Hotspur and Arsenal both therefore missed out as a result, despite finishing in seventh and ninth positions respectively.

And when eighth-place finishers West Bromwich Albion beat Everton in the FA Cup Final to take a spot in the European Cup Winners' Cup competition, the fourth and final Fairs Cup place was Newcastle's.

Had the result been reversed and Everton won the FA Cup, the Toffees would have gone into the Cup Winners' Cup and West Brom would have taken the final Fairs Cup place rather than Newcastle. So, indirectly, the man Magpies fans have to thank for their Fairs Cup triumph is West Brom striker Jeff Astle, scorer of the only goal in the 1968 FA Cup Final.

— PREMIER LEAGUE RECORD —

By the end of the 2011/12 season Newcastle United had played 692 Premiership games, winning 277 of those, drawing 186 and losing 229.

Home:	Played	Won	Drawn	Lost
	346	186	88	72
Away:	Played	Won	Drawn	Lost
	346	91	98	157

In these games the Magpies have scored 996 goals and conceded 885.

— TWIN TOWERS PART I —

One year after the famous 'White Horse Final' of 1923, Newcastle made their first appearance at the new Empire Stadium – with both players and supporters finding it rather to their liking. Here are the club's results at Wembley up to and including Newcastle's last FA Cup win in 1955:

April 27th 1924   FA Cup Final   Won 2–0 against Aston Villa
Newcastle team: William Bradley, Billy Hampson, Frank Hudspeth, Edward Mooney, Charlie Spencer, Willie Gibson, James Low, Willie Cowan, Neil Harris, Tommy McDonald, Stan Seymour
Scorers: Seymour, Harris

April 23rd 1932   FA Cup Final   Won 2–1 against Arsenal
Albert McInroy, Jimmy Nelson, David Fairhurst, Roddie Mackenzie, Dave Davidson, Sammy Weaver, Jimmy Boyd, Jimmy Richardson, Jack Allen, Harry McMenemy, Tommy Lang
Scorer: Allen (2)

April 28th 1951   FA Cup Final   Won 2–0 against Blackpool
Jack Fairbrother, Bobby Cowell, Bobby Corbett, Joe Harvey, Frank Brennan, Charlie Crowe, Tommy Walker, Ernie Taylor, Jackie Milburn, George Robledo, Bobby Mitchell
Scorer: Milburn (2)

April 3rd 1952   FA Cup Final   Won 1–0 against Arsenal
Ronnie Simpson, Bobby Cowell, Alf McMichael, Joe Harvey, Frank Brennan, Ted Robledo, Tommy Walker, Bill Foulkes, Jackie Milburn, George Robledo, Bobby Mitchell
Scorer: G. Robledo

May 22nd 1955   FA Cup Final   Won 3–1 against Manchester City
Ronnie Simpson, Bobby Cowell, Ron Batty, Jimmy Scoular, Bob Stokoe, Tommy Casey, Len White, Jackie Milburn, Vic Keeble, George Hannah, Bobby Mitchell
Scorers: Milburn, Mitchell, Hannah

A local newspaper reporter described the crowd's reaction to Jackie Milburn's second goal in 1951 as follows:

"The Geordies seemed to want to jump right into Heaven. The spectacle was a study of mass delirium, a black and white sketch of mass hysteria in its most nerve-shattering form."

— NEWCASTLE LEGENDS: LEN WHITE —

Yorkshire grit in black and white

Newcastle's failure to appear in a third successive FA Cup Final in 1953 had one silver lining, Len White being signed from Rotherham just days after he had inspired the Millers to a 3–1 fourth round victory at Gallowgate.

The 22-year-old Yorkshireman cost £12,500 and spent the early part of his Newcastle career operating on the right flank, while still working as a miner at Burradon Colliery.

However, White's reputation as one of the best uncapped players of the era was built on his performances for the Magpies at centre forward after the departures of Jackie Milburn and Vic Keeble.

A run of stylish free-scoring displays made White a genuine crowd favourite, although inconsistency elsewhere in the side often meant that his efforts up front were nullified by defensive lapses.

White's sole honour was a 1955 FA Cup Winner's medal – a game in which he delivered the corner for Jackie Milburn to head home against Manchester City in the opening seconds at Wembley. Untimely cup exits at the hands of the likes of Millwall and Scunthorpe United were to follow in subsequent seasons, though, while his haul of 22 goals in 30 league appearances in 1957/58 was only enough to see the club narrowly avoid relegation.

Had White played for a London club, an England call-up would have been likely. As it was though, his appearance for a Football League XI in November 1958 gave a hint of what his country missed. Playing against an Irish League side at Anfield, White scored three goals in eight second-half minutes during a 5–2 victory.

However, like Tony Green a decade later, injury was to overshadow White's career. A challenge by Tottenham's Dave Mackay at White Hart Lane in March 1961 took the gloss off a 2–1 victory against the team who would complete the Double within weeks. Sidelined for six months with ruptured ankle ligaments, by the time White returned to the Magpies line-up they were in Division Two and manager Charlie Mitten was about to be jettisoned, as his side struggled to mount a promotion bid.

It was evident that the injury had robbed White of his pace and in February 1962 he returned to his native Yorkshire, joining Huddersfield as the makeweight in a deal which took Scottish forward Jimmy Kerray to St James' Park.

After being belatedly rewarded for his efforts for the club with a testimonial game in 1989 (held at Whitley Bay after Newcastle United scandalously refused to take part), cancer claimed White in 1994 at the age of 64.

While Jackie Milburn remains synonymous with United's 1950s achievements, Len White is something of a forgotten hero.

Len White factfile
Born: Skellow, March 23rd 1930   Died: June 17th 1994
Newcastle career: 270 apps, 153 goals (1953–62)
Other clubs: Rotherham, Huddersfield, Stockport County

— GOD BLESS HER . . . AND ALL
WHO SAIL IN HER —

Her Majesty The Queen's Coronation in June 1953 saw the eyes of the world turn to Westminster Abbey, while celebratory events took place across Great Britain and beyond. Newcastle United's contribution to proceedings was to participate in an eight-team invitational tournament involving Scottish and English clubs in May 1953, which was, in effect, an unofficial British club championship.

Scottish double winners Rangers, league runners-up Hibernian and beaten cup finalists Aberdeen represented Scotland – with Celtic making up the numbers. Making the trip over the border to Glasgow, meanwhile, were league champions Arsenal, plus Manchester United and Tottenham Hotspur – who had finished in pole position in the two previous seasons. 1951 and 1952 FA Cup winners Newcastle completed the line-up, with Blackpool overlooked, despite winning at Wembley less than two weeks previously.

The Coronation Cup began with Hibs and Spurs drawing 1–1 at Ibrox Park and Celtic beating Arsenal 1–0 at Hampden Park – Gateshead-born Bill Dodgin featuring for the Gunners. With extra time having failed to separate the sides, Hibernian then returned to Ibrox the following day to beat Spurs 2–1. The English then hit back, with Manchester United overcoming Rangers 2–1 at Hampden and Newcastle scoring four without reply against Aberdeen in front of 16,000 fans at Ibrox.

Team: Ronnie Simpson, Ron Batty, Bobby Cowell, Joe Harvey, Frank Brennan, Charlie Crowe, Len White, Tommy Mulgrew, Jackie Milburn, George Hannah, Bobby Mitchell.

Scorers: Milburn, White, Hannah, OG (Alec Young)

The semi-finals then saw a 2–1 win for Celtic over Manchester United at Hampden, but hopes of a cross-border final evaporated, with 48,876 fans witnessing Newcastle end up on the wrong end of a 0–4 scoreline against Hibs at Ibrox.

United fielded the same XI as had beaten Aberdeen four days earlier but were undone by the Easter Road "Famous Five" forward line of Gordon Smith, Bobby Johnstone, Lawrie Reilly, Eddie Turnbull and Willie Ormond. Reilly led the way with two goals, while Turnbull and Johnstone notched one apiece.

The Coronation Cup was then won by Celtic, goals from Neil Mochan and Jimmy Walsh giving them a 2–0 victory over Hibernian in front of 107,060 fans at Hampden.

— IT'S A KNOCKOUT —

While no TV coverage of the FA Cup would be complete without footage of 'that' Ronnie Radford goal from 1972, the 'Nightmare on Edgar Street' is by no means the only occasion on which the Magpies have exited from the competition at the hands of lower league opposition.

In the 55 seasons since the resumption of the competition in 1946, United have been humbled by supposedly inferior sides on no fewer than 21 occasions – 11 of those coming in front of disbelieving crowds on Tyneside:

Season	Opponent	Score	Feat
1948/49	Bradford Park Ave (h)	0–2	Division 3 beat Division 1
1956/57	Millwall (a)	1–2	Division 3 South beat Division 1
1957/58	Scunthorpe United (h)	1–3	Division 3 North beat Division 1
1960/61	Sheffield United (h)	1–3	Division 2 beat Division 1
1961/62	Peterborough (h)	0–1	Division 3 beat Division 2
1963/64	Bedford Town (h)	1–2	Non-League beat Division 2
1967/68	Carlisle United (h)	0–1	Division 2 beat Division 1
1971/72	Hereford United (a)	1–2	Non-League beat Division 1
1972/73	Luton Town (a)	0–2	Division 2 beat Division 1
1974/75	Walsall (a)	0–1	Division 3 beat Division 1
1977/78	Wrexham (a)	1–4	Division 3 beat Division 1
1979/80	Chester City (h)	0–2	Division 3 beat Division 2
1980/81	Exeter City (a)	0–4	Division 3 beat Division 2
1985/86	Brighton & Hove Albion (h)	0–2	Division 2 beat Division 1
1988/89	Watford (a)	0–1	Division 2 beat Division 1
1991/92	AFC Bournemouth (h)	3–4	Division 3 beat Division 2 (on pens)
1993/94	Luton Town (a)	0–2	Division 1 beat Premier League
2002/03	Wolverhampton Wanderers (a)	2–3	Division 1 beat Premier League
2006/07	Birmingham City (h)	1–5	Championship beat Premier League
2010/11	Stevenage (a)	1–3	League Two beat Premier League
2011/12	Brighton & Hove Albion (a)	0–1	Championship beat Premier League

— DOUBLE RATIONS —

The once traditional scheduling of League fixtures on both Christmas Day and Boxing Day last saw Newcastle United in action on December 25th and 26th back in 1957.

On Christmas Day Nottingham Forest visited Tyneside and triumphed 4–1 in front of 25,214 spectators. United gained revenge, though, 24 hours later on the banks of the Trent, winning 3–2 at the City Ground watched by a crowd of 32,359.

Some fixtures were scheduled on December 25th in both 1958 and 1959 before the practice was finally discontinued. However, Newcastle didn't have games on Christmas Day in either season.

— LEAGUE OF NATIONS —

By the end of the 2011/12 season, no fewer than 171 players from 41 different countries had represented Newcastle United in their 18 seasons of Premier League football.

Country	Player Total
England	69
France	19
Scotland	8
Republic of Ireland	9
Senegal	5
Wales	5
Argentina	4
Northern Ireland	4
Spain	4
Italy	3
Netherlands	3

Plus double representation from: Australia, Brazil, Czech Republic, Democratic Republic of Congo, Denmark, Greece, Nigeria and Portugal. Single representatives have come from Belgium, Cameroon, Canada, Chile, Colombia, Croatia, Cyprus, Finland, Georgia, Germany, Ivory Coast, Norway, Paraguay, Peru, Slovenia, South Africa, Sweden, Switzerland, Trinidad & Tobago, Turkey, the United States of America and Uruguay. Of those 171 players, 29 came through the ranks from the club's own Academy.

International affiliation rather than country of birth has been taken as a measure, for example Shefki Kuqi was born in the former

Yugoslavia but played for Finland. Four players have also made Premier League appearances for the club in separate spells – Tommy Wright, Robbie Elliott, Lee Clark and Pavel Srnicek. These players are only counted once in the above totals.

— BRIEF ENCOUNTERS I —

A selection of overseas players who spent time on trial with Newcastle United but never made a competitive appearance for the club:

Player	Country of Birth
Hamed Kavianpour	Iran
Joonas Kolka	Finland
Yoann Lachor	France
Dennis Lawrence	Trinidad
Erwin Lemmens	Belgium
Dragan Lukic	Yugoslavia
Ernest Mtawali	Malawi
Markus Munch	Germany
Nicki Bille Nielsen	Denmark
Victor Nogueira	Portugal
Massimo Oddo	Italy
Isaac Okoronkwo	Nigeria
Pietro Parente	Italy
Pablo Paz	Argentina
Bruno Pereira	Portugal
Bachirou Salou	Togo
Christian Schwegler	Switzerland
Diaby Sekana	Ivory Coast
Tariq	Libya
Shalom Tikva	Israel
Diego Tur	Denmark
Frank Wiblishauser	Germany
Ray Xuerub	Malta
Marc Ziegler	Germany
Chris Zoricich	New Zealand

— NEWCASTLE LEGENDS: SHAY GIVEN —

Shay Given: already a Toon legend

Shay Given celebrated a decade with Newcastle United in May 2007, having been bought from Blackburn for £1.5 million by his former Rovers boss Kenny Dalglish. Dalglish had first spotted the goalkeeper's potential when he was a teenager at Celtic, signing Given for Blackburn in 1994.

Having being loaned to both Swindon Town and Sunderland (who it was rumoured were unable to fund a permanent transfer), Given tussled with Steve Harper for the position of first-choice goalkeeper at St James Park for a number of seasons.

The Irish international took pole position in the 2000/01 campaign, missing just four Premiership fixtures as he established himself in the side after withdrawing a hastily submitted transfer request.

During that season, Given began a run of 140 consecutive Premiership appearances at Leeds in January 2001, making 100 per cent appearance records in the following three seasons. That impressive run was broken in October 2004 when Given remained on Tyneside as his wife gave birth – Steve Harper deputising away at Bolton.

By the end of the 2007/08 season, Given had risen to fourth in Newcastle's all-time appearance table (see *Familiar Faces*, page 40) and with a contract keeping him on Tyneside until 2011, he has a great chance of becoming the first Magpie ever to reach the 500 mark.

An outstanding shot-stopper, Given's importance to Newcastle was recognised by then manager Glenn Roeder when he was appointed captain following the retirement of Alan Shearer in the summer of 2006. Shortly after taking the skipper's armband, however, Given was involved in a sickening collision at West Ham United in September 2006 which left him with abdominal injuries that the surgeon who operated on him likened to those suffered by car crash victims. He returned to action after two months to put in some excellent performances, but ended another season having seen his efforts undermined by the shortcomings of those players in front of him.

Like all goalkeepers, Given has had a few moments he would prefer to forget – none more so than the goal he conceded against Coventry at Highfield Road in November 1997. In an initially innocuous piece of play, Given claimed possession of the ball on the edge of his six-yard box and threw the ball down in front of him in preparation for clearing it downfield. However, as a number of reporters later wryly observed, he was the only Irishman who didn't know where Dublin was – Coventry striker Dion Dublin appearing from behind him and scoring a perfectly legitimate goal by tapping the loose ball into the Newcastle net.

A far better memory for Given was being awarded the captain's armband by Ireland boss Steve Staunton in March 2007, leading his side out at Dublin's Croke Park against Slovakia. That honour came on the occasion of Given's 80th full international cap, which equalled the previous Ireland record for a goalkeeper, held by Packie Bonner.

Sadly, Given reached the point of no return at St James' Park midway through the club's relegation campaign of 2008/09 and moved on to Manchester City during the January transfer window. By July 2011 he was an Aston Villa player, having gained an FA Cup winners' medal as a non-playing substitute at Wembley three months earlier.

Shay Given factfile
Born: April 20th 1976, Lifford, County Donegal
Newcastle career: 463 apps (1997–2009)
Other clubs: Celtic, Blackburn Rovers, Swindon Town (loan), Sunderland (loan), Manchester City, Aston Villa.
International: Republic of Ireland, 121 caps

— TWIN TOWERS PART II —

Venue of Legends for some, Wembley Stadium has proved to be nothing but an arena of misery for Newcastle supporters since the club's last success there in 1955. As Alan Shearer commented in 2002, 'for Newcastle United, the sooner they knock down this place the better'.

May 4th 1974   FA Cup Final   Lost 0–3 to Liverpool
Newcastle team: Iam McFaul, Frank Clark, Alan Kennedy, Terry McDermott, Pat Howard, Bobby Moncur, Jimmy Smith (Tommy Gibb), Tommy Cassidy, Malcolm Macdonald, John Tudor, Terry Hibbitt.

February 28th 1976 League Cup Final Lost 1–2 to Manchester City
Mick Mahoney, Irving Nattrass, Alan Kennedy, Stewart Barrowclough, Glen Keely, Pat Howard, Mickey Burns, Tommy Cassidy, Malcolm Macdonald, Alan Gowling, Tommy Craig. Substitute unused: Paul Cannell.
Scorer: Gowling.

August 11th 1996 FA Charity Shield Lost 0–4 to Manchester United
Pavel Srnicek, Steve Watson, Darren Peacock, Philippe Albert, John Beresford, David Batty, Robert Lee, Peter Beardsley (Tino Asprilla), Alan Shearer, Les Ferdinand, David Ginola (Keith Gillespie). Substitutes unused: Shaka Hislop, Warren Barton, Steve Howey, Lee Clark, Paul Kitson.

May 16th 1998   FA Cup Final   Lost 0–2 to Arsenal
Shay Given, Stuart Pearce (Andreas Andersson), Steve Howey, Nicos Dabizas, Alessandro Pistone, Gary Speed, David Batty, Robert Lee, Alan Shearer, Temuri Ketsbaia (John Barnes), Warren Barton (Steve Watson). Substitutes unused: Shaka Hislop, Philippe Albert.

May 22nd 1999   FA Cup Final   Lost 0–2 to Manchester United
Steve Harper, Andy Griffin, Laurent Charvet, Nicos Dabizas, Didier Domi, Robert Lee, Didi Hamann (Duncan Ferguson), Gary Speed, Alan Shearer, Temuri Ketsbaia (Glass), Nolberto Solano (Silvio Maric). Substitutes unused: Shay Given, Warren Barton, Stephen Glass.

April 9th 2000   FA Cup Semi-final   Lost 1–2 to Chelsea
Shay Given, Warren Barton, Steve Howey, Nicos Dabizas, Aaron Hughes (Temuri Ketsbaia), Robert Lee, Gary Speed, Kieron Dyer, Alan Shearer, Duncan Ferguson (Didier Domi), Nolberto Solano. Substitutes unused: Steve Harper, Alain Goma, Diego Gavilan. Scorer: Lee.

— STATUESQUE I —

Never mind the edifice that confronts travellers approaching Tyneside from the south, through black-and-white eyes the true Angel of the North statue is one depicting Magpies hero Jackie Milburn, who died in 1988.

The question is, though, which statue?

Statue number one was created in bronze by Susanna Robinson and was unveiled in November 1991 by Wor Jackie's widow, Laura, at a site on Northumberland Street in Newcastle city centre. The statue is 1.8m high.

Costing £35K and paid for via public subscription, the statue was removed in 1998 ahead of pedestrianisation works and relocated to a new site on St James' Boulevard (to the West of St James' Park) in June 1999.

The bronze football accompanying the statue was stolen and replaced on numerous occasions while displayed on Northumberland Street – found on one occasion in nearby Jesmond Dene by a dog (almost certainly not called Pickles) in 1996.

Following talks between Newcastle City Council, the football club and the Milburn family, April 2012 then saw the statue brought "home" to St James' Park. It now stands by the South East corner of the stadium at the Gallowgate End, where Milburn himself requested his ashes be scattered.

Statue number two was sculpted in bronze by John W. Mills, this stands 2.4m high and was also erected by public subscription. It's positioned on Station Road in Wor Jackie's hometown of Ashington, Northumberland, and was unveiled in October 1995 by Laura Milburn.

Statue number three was designed by sculptor Tom Maley for consideration as the Ashington Milburn statue, only for the Mills entry to be commissioned.

Undaunted, locally-born Maley constructed the 1.8m statue in fibreglass and it went on temporary display at Woodhorn Colliery Museum in Ashington.

Following the intervention of Newcastle United Chairman Sir John Hall (who was born nearby), the club paid for a pedestal on which the statue was mounted outside the South West corner of St James' Park and unveiled in December 1996.

Talk that that Maley would be commissioned to reproduce the statue in bronze, however, never bore fruit and it was removed in February 1999 as reconstruction of the stadium continued. It hasn't been seen in public since.

PS: A bust of Wor Jackie is also on display in the Old Milburn

Reception area of St James' Park, along with his trio of FA Cup winners' medals from the 1950s.

— TRANSFER TRAIL I —

In chronological order, Newcastle United's record purchases have been as follows:

Player	Year	Fee	Paid to
Bobby Templeton	1903	£400	Aston Villa
Andy McCombie	1904	£700	Sunderland
George Wilson	1907	£1,600	Everton
Billy Hibbert	1911	£1,950	Bury
Neil Harris	1920	£3,300	Partick Thistle
Hughie Gallacher	1925	£6,500	Airdrieonians
Jack Hill	1928	£8,100	Burnley
Harry Clifton	1938	£8,500	Chesterfield
Len Shackleton	1946	£13,000	Bradford Park Avenue
George Lowrie	1948	£18,500	Coventry City
Jimmy Scoular	1953	£22,250	Portsmouth
Ivor Allchurch	1958	£28,000	Swansea Town
Barrie Thomas	1962	£45,000	Scunthorpe United
Wyn Davies	1966	£80,000	Bolton Wanderers
Jimmy Smith	1969	£100,000	Aberdeen
Malcolm Macdonald	1971	£180,000	Luton Town
Peter Withe	1978	£200,000	Nottingham Forest
John Trewick	1980	£250,000	West Bromwich Albion
Paul Goddard	1986	£415,000	West Ham United
Mirandinha	1987	£575,000	Palmeiras
John Robertson	1988	£750,000	Heart of Midlothian
Dave Beasant	1988	£850,000	Wimbledon
Andy Thorn	1988	£850,000	Wimbledon
Andy Cole	1993	£1,750,000	Bristol City
Ruel Fox	1995	£2,225,000	Norwich City
Darren Peacock	1995	£2,700,000	Queens Park Rangers
Les Ferdinand	1995	£6,000,000	Queens Park Rangers
Tino Asprilla	1996	£7,500,000	Parma
Alan Shearer	1996	£15,000,000	Blackburn Rovers
Michael Owen	2005	£16,000,000	Real Madrid

— INTERNATIONAL APPEARANCES —

The current holder of the club's international appearance record is Shay Given, who broke the record on April 30th 2003 when playing for the Republic of Ireland against Norway.

A clean sheet that night in a 1–0 win at Lansdowne Road marked the 50th senior cap of the goalkeeper's career and the 41st earned whilst a Newcastle player. In doing so he broke the previous 40-game tally of Northern Ireland's Alf McMichael – a record that had stood for some 43 years.

Since then, Given has extended the record further, reaching 86 caps for Ireland (and therefore 77 as a Magpie) in February 2008. McMichael's tally was also subsequently bettered by Greek defender Nicos Dabizas and Northern Ireland's Aaron Hughes. Shay went on to extend that record further to 81 caps against Poland at Croke Park in November 2008, before completing a transfer to Manchester, early the following year.

Newcastle United's top ten international appearance makers:

Rank	Player	Total	Country
1	Shay Given	81	Republic of Ireland
2	Nicos Dabizas	43	Greece
3	Aaron Hughes	41	Northern Ireland
4	Alf McMichael	40	Northern Ireland
5	Gary Speed	36	Wales
6	Alan Shearer	35	England
7	Kieron Dyer	32	England
8	Nolberto Solano	28	Peru
9=	Peter Beardsley	25	England
9=	David Craig	25	Northern Ireland
10	Dick Keith	23	Northern Ireland

Note: Only caps gained whilst a Newcastle player are included in this list.

— NEWCASTLE LEGENDS: MALCOLM MACDONALD —

TOON LEGENDS

MALCOLM MACDONALD

Supermac!

One of the finest strikers in Newcastle's illustrious history, Malcolm Macdonald was signed from Luton Town in 1971 for £180,000 by Toon boss Joe Harvey to solve a goalscoring problem.

Arriving at St James' Park in a hired Rolls Royce exuding brashness and confidence, Macdonald had a similar swagger on the pitch. In his five years on Tyneside he scored many memorable goals, beginning with a hat-trick against Liverpool on his home league debut. Fast and powerful, Macdonald possessed an explosive left foot and many of his best strikes – like his rocket shot at home to Leicester City that has gone down in folklore as one of the best ever seen at

Gallowgate – gave the opposition keeper absolutely no chance of making a save.

The goals kept on coming, but the writing was on the wall for Macdonald when Harvey was replaced by Gordon Lee, a cautious manager who advocated a strict 'no stars' policy. Relations between club and player soon deteriorated, with an eventual parting of the ways coming in August 1976 when Arsenal shelled out £333,333 to take him to Highbury.

A parallel can be drawn between Macdonald and his eventual successor in the number nine shirt Alan Shearer. Both were to leave Newcastle without winners' medals or goals in either of their two cup final appearances. However, both enjoyed some happy moments in the semi-finals that led to those Wembley appearances, Macdonald scoring twice against Burnley in 1974 at Hillsborough in front of a fevered Newcastle support.

And like Shearer, Macdonald now earns a living as a football pundit, appearing at talk-ins and on a regular radio phone-in programme in the North East. Both have sampled football management, with Malcolm's tenure at Fulham showing signs of promise before disintegrating in the fall-out from a controversial game with Derby County that blighted hopes of promotion for the Cottagers. Later, in an eight-month spell at Huddersfield, his side was on the wrong end of a confidence-shattering 10–1 league defeat away at Manchester City. After his management career ended, Macdonald experienced a number of setbacks in his business and personal life and for a while was a self-confessed alcoholic.

Happily a PFA-funded knee operation in 1997 sent Malcolm on the road to recovery and sobriety.

Malcolm Macdonald factfile
Born: Fulham, January 7th 1950
Newcastle career: 228 apps, 121 goals (1971–76)
Other clubs: Fulham, Luton Town, Arsenal
International: England, 14 caps, 6 goals

— GOLD STANDARD —

Nineteen players have appeared in World Cup finals while their registration was held by Newcastle United. They are:

Year	Host	Player	Nation
1950	Brazil	Jackie Milburn	England
1950	Brazil	George Robledo	Chile
1954	Switzerland	Ivor Broadis	England
1958	Sweden	Tommy Casey	Northern Ireland
1958	Sweden	Dick Keith	Northern Ireland
1958	Sweden	Alf McMichael	Northern Ireland
1986	Mexico	Peter Beardsley	England
1986	Mexico	David McCreery	Northern Ireland
1986	Mexico	Ian Stewart	Northern Ireland
1990	Italy	Roy Aitken	Scotland
1998	France	David Batty	England
1998	France	Robert Lee	England
1998	France	Alan Shearer	England
2002	Japan/South Korea	Kieron Dyer	England
2002	Japan/South Korea	Diego Gavilan	Paraguay
2002	Japan/South Korea	Shay Given	Republic of Ireland
2006	Germany	Michael Owen	England
2006	Germany	Craig Moore	Australia
2010	South Africa	Jonas Gutierrez	Argentina

In addition, Stephane Guivarc'h officially signed for Newcastle 24 hours after becoming a World Cup winner with France in 1998. The striker made his sixth appearance of the tournament in the final against Brazil, but failed to score in any of them. His lack of form attracted the attention of TV pundits including a certain Ruud Gullit, who was somewhat disparaging. Little did Gullit know though that within a matter of weeks he would be Guivarc'h's manager at St James' Park.

— MEMORY MATCHES 2 —

April 21st 1986

West Ham United 8 Newcastle United 1 (Division One)

A midweek visit to Upton Park saw a mid-table Newcastle suffering a goalkeeping injury crisis, with reserve custodian Dave McKellar sustaining a hip injury during a 1–1 draw at Chelsea the previous weekend. Manager Willie McFaul resisted the temptation to come out of retirement and chose to field first-choice Martin Thomas between the posts, despite suffering shoulder problems. That decision rapidly backfired though, as defender Alvin Martin netted from close range within five minutes. And by half time, Thomas had been beaten three times more, parrying Ray Stewart's right wing cross into his own net before allowing a Neil Orr effort from distance to slip through his gloves. Magpies skipper (and future Hammers boss) Glenn Roeder then added insult to injury with a farcical OG, inexplicably back-flicking the ball into the corner of his own net from six yards out. In the days before substitute goalkeepers, winger Ian Stewart appeared at the interval and rookie Chris Hedworth went in goal – only to then damage his collarbone almost immediately when fouled by Tony Cottee. A soft header from Martin then gave him his second of the night to make it 5–0, before the brave Hedworth resumed outfield duties and Peter Beardsley donned the green jersey. A low Billy Whitehurst shot at the other end was then cleared from behind the line to make it 5–1, before Newcastle were reduced to ten men when Hedworth limped off and Hammers substitute Paul Goddard beat Beardsley with a point-blank header at the far post. Frank McAvennie then quickly added another headed effort, before an inexplicable penalty was awarded against Roeder. Despite losing 1–7 with six minutes remaining at that point, half a dozen visiting players surrounded the referee and it took the presence of police officers at pitchside to calm the furious protests.West Ham's usual penalty taker Ray Stewart initially shaped to take the kick, but with the Upton Park crowd chanting "Alvin, Alvin", the ball was handed to Martin and he duly sent Beardsley the wrong way with a right-footed effort; completing the feat of netting a hat trick against three different players (calling them goalkeepers is pushing the grounds of credibility rather too far).

NUFC: Thomas (Stewart), McDonald, Bailey, McCreery, Anderson, Roeder, Stephenson, Hedworth, Whitehurst, Beardsley, Cunningham.

— LOCAL FILMS FOR LOCAL PEOPLE —

The treasure trove of Victorian documentary film footage unearthed in a Blackburn shop during 1994 excited movie buffs and social historians alike – and provided a hitherto unseen archive of English football in the early 20th century.

Amongst 800 films totalling 28 hours shot by and in conjunction with the Mitchell and Kenyon Company was footage of 32 football matches played between 1901 and 1907.

Intended to be shown at venues including local halls and travelling shows, the commercial intent of these films lay in allowing "ordinary people" to see themselves on screen. Thus, the footage shot tended towards street scenes and mass gatherings, with the football films focusing as much on the banks of spectators as the on-field participants.

As one of the higher-profile sides of the era, Newcastle United featured in three films; cameras visiting St James' Park on one occasion – one of only a handful of excursions away from the North West of England:

November 23rd 1901 Newcastle 1 Liverpool 0

Only the second-ever football match covered by Mitchell and Kenyon (after Liverpool versus Small Heath), Manchester-based showman Arthur Duncan Thomas commissioned the filming of this game.

Utilising four separate cameras (one covering the teams entering the field, one providing crowd scenes and two for the actual game), a 1–0 home win was recorded thanks to a Bob McColl goal.

September 13th 1902 Everton 0 Newcastle 1

The Magpies emerged triumphant from this visit to Goodison Park (which had been open barely ten years) thanks to a strike from Willie Stewart.

September 19th 1903 Everton 4 Newcastle 1

A Jimmy Howie effort was no more than a consolation as the Toffees netted through messrs Booth, Hardman, Settle and Young.

Given their first public airing in the region for a century at Newcastle's Tyneside Cinema in 2005, the football films were accompanied by footage including scenes of bathers at Tynemouth, the Armstrong factory in Elswick, North Shields Fish Quay and a horse-drawn fire engine in the city.

The FA Cup first round draw of January 1907 then presented Mitchell and Kenyon with an opportunity to film ties on both Tyneside and Wearside. Despite being commissioned by Tyneside-based cinema manager Ralph, the cameras headed off to Roker Park to cover Sunderland's 4–1 victory over Leicester Fosse.

No footage, therefore, exists of United's 0–1 loss to Southern League Crystal Palace – a genuine giant-killing feat – and the name of scorer Horace Astley languishes in obscurity.

Regrettably, the BBC chose not to follow this example when the

Magpies played fellow Southern League team Hereford United in the same competition, some 65 years later . . .

— LONDON CALLING —

Saturday 2nd September 1893 saw both Newcastle United and Woolwich Arsenal play their first-ever Football League fixtures, the sides meeting at the Manor Ground in Plumstead, South East London.

However it proved to be a testing debut in the capital for the team from Tyneside who had arrived at Kings Cross by train early on the morning of the game having been unable to afford hotel accommodation.

The teams lined up as follows:

Woolwich Arsenal: Williams, Powell, Jeffrey, Devine, Buist, Howat, Gemmell, Henderson, Shaw, Elliott, Booth.

Newcastle United: Ramsay, Jeffrey, Miller, Crielly, Graham, McKane, Bowman, Crate, Thompson, Sorley, Wallace.

With Newcastle trailing at the interval to a Shaw effort, Arsenal quickly doubled the lead through Elliott. However goals from Tom Crate and Jock Sorley gave Newcastle a point (some contemporary reports crediting Willie Graham as scoring Newcastle's opener).

— SHEAR CLASS —

Alan Shearer is the Premiership's highest ever scorer, closely followed by one Andrew Cole. In fact, four of the Premiership's top scorers have notched a fair few of their tally in the black and white stripes off Newcastle United.

Premier League Top Ten goalscorers:

Player	Total	For Newcastle
Alan Shearer	260	148
Andy Cole	189	43
Thierry Henry	176	0
Robbie Fowler	163	0
Michael Owen	149	26
Les Ferdinand	149	41
Frank Lampard	149	0
Teddy Sheringham	147	0

| Wayne Rooney | 144 | 0 |
| Jimmy Floyd Hasselbaink | 127 | 0 |

— FLYING THE FLAG PART I —

Newcastle United's Joe Rogers has the distinction of being the club's very first international player, featuring in a ground-breaking representative tour organised by the English Football Association in November 1899.

The previously uncapped Rogers was part of a 14-man squad who played four games in just six days against German and Austrian opposition.

The tour came at the suggestion of one Walter Bensemann, a 26-year-old German football enthusiast, who wrote to the FA and then travelled to London to state his case – winning approval due in part to his flawless command of English and also his willingness to meet the £200 cost of the tour.

Opening with a 13–2 win over Germany in Berlin, the two sides met again at the same venue less than 24 hours later, with the FA this time only capable of a 10–2 conquest (reportedly due to a late-night drinking session). Five of those ten goals were scored by Rogers – who presumably had an early night.

Boarding a train to Prague immediately after that game, an 8–0 victory over a joint German-Austrian XI was recorded there, before the tour ended with a 7–0 success against a different German select side in Karlsruhe. Missing two club matches (during which United failed to score), Joe appeared in three of the four FA games and netted seven times in total. However, he was never to be capped formally by England and would later move to Germany to work as a coach.

Subsequent FA tours of South Africa in both 1910 and 1920 didn't feature any Newcastle players (although former Magpie Bob Benson was in the 1910 party). United were then represented by both Stan Seymour and Charlie Spencer as the FA toured Australia in 1925 with a 17-man squad.

A mammoth 25 games were played between late May and early August – including five "Test matches" against the Australian nation team – the visitors ending up with a 100 per cent record and scoring 139 goals in the process. Traversing the country, the party stopped off twice in the New South Wales city of Newcastle, beating Northern Districts 6–0 in mid-June before returning early the following month for a 3–0 win over a hometown XI.

Spencer was back in a Newcastle shirt for their second league game of the following season in early September 1925, but Seymour didn't feature for another month, and he celebrated his return to Magpies action with two goals in a 7–0 demolition of Arsenal at St James' Park in early October. And even then, their FA commitments weren't over, with both Spencer and Seymour featuring as the FA side contested the 1925/26 FA Charity Shield 48 hours after that Arsenal victory. Hardly surprisingly, their Amateur opponents were in much better nick and ran up a 6–1 scoreline at White Hart Lane.

Fast forward to 1978 and Ipswich Town Manager Bobby Robson was tasked with leading what was officially an England "B" Team tour of Malaysia, New Zealand and Singapore. Included in his party was Magpies defender Alan Kennedy, while Leyton Orient defender Glenn Roeder would later play and manage at St James' Park and David Geddis serve on Robson's backroom team at Gallowgate many years later.

Winning his second "B" cap, Kennedy netted in the tour opener as England drew 1–1 with Malaysia in Kuala Lumpur. And the Magpie was on the scoresheet again in the tour-closing 8–0 rout of Singapore in the National Stadium.

— SHOLA THE DEMON QUELLER —

By the end of the season, Newcastle striker Shola Ameobi had featured in no less than a dozen Tyne Wear derby matches in the Premier League – and finished on the losing side just once. Here's his appearance and scoring record:

2000/01	drew 1–1 (a)	Substitute
2001/02	drew 1–1(h)	Started
2001/02	won 1–0 (a)	Substitute
2002/03	won 2–0 (h)	Substitute
2002/03	won 1–0 (a)	Substitute
2005/06	won 3–2 (h)	Started – scored twice
2008/09	lost 1–2 (a)	Started – scored once
2008/09	drew 1–1 (h)	Started – scored once (penalty)
2010/11	won 5–1 (h)	Started – scored twice (1 penalty)
2010/11	drew 1–1 (a)	Started
2011/12	won 1–0 (a)	Started
2011/12	drew 1–1 (h)	Substitute – scored once

Those seven goals put United's number 23 third in the club's all-time derby scorer's list, with only Jackie Milburn (11) and Albert Shepherd (9) ahead of him. However Shola's twelve outings in these games is some way off the gargantuan total of 27 amassed by Magpies goalkeeper, Jimmy Lawrence.

— NEWCASTLE LEGENDS: ALAN SHEARER —

Shearer, Shearer!

It is something of a minor tragedy that Alan Shearer ended his career with a single honour, the Premiership winner's medal he collected with Blackburn Rovers.

A one-time schoolboy trialist with Newcastle – contrary to urban myth he only played briefly in goal during his trial – Shearer began his professional career at Southampton before making a big money move to Blackburn in 1992. At Ewood Park his forceful centre forward play and powerful shooting were key factors in the Lancashire side's 1995 title success. However, a year later, after spurning offers from Manchester United, Arsenal and Barcelona, Shearer was persuaded by Kevin Keegan to return to his Geordie roots.

Twenty-five goals in 31 Premiership games earned a second successive runner's up spot for his new club, despite the shock mid-season departure of his teenage hero Keegan (a young Shearer can be seen acting as ball boy in footage of Keegan's testimonial).

His second season at the club began badly when he was seriously injured in a pre-season tournament at Goodison Park in August 1997.

He returned to action to fire the club into successive FA Cup finals in 1998 and 1999, only to end up on the losing side on both occasions.

Despite his goals and clear commitment to the Newcastle cause, both Ruud Gullit and Sir Bobby Robson subsequently attempted to dislodge Shearer from his perch as the uncrowned King of Tyneside – the former by controversially leaving him out of the side against Sunderland, the latter attempting to sell him to Liverpool.

Shearer outlasted both managers, though, and postponed his planned retirement after talks with their successor Graham Souness in 2005. His decision to carry on playing enabled him to set a new Newcastle scoring record. Goal number 200 against Mansfield Town in the FA Cup at St James' Park in January 2006 equalled Jackie Milburn's tally and a month later he claimed the record outright against Portsmouth.

Shearer's goals during this period helped another new manager – caretaker boss Glenn Roeder – to a winning start, amid widespread speculation that Roeder was merely keeping the seat warm for the popular Magpies' skipper.

A revitalised Newcastle rose into the top half of the table in the second half of the 2005/06 season, with a trip to Sunderland giving Shearer more reason to celebrate as he helped his side come from behind by scoring goal number 206.

However, within ten minutes of scoring from the spot, Shearer's playing career was over – caught accidentally in the tackle by Julio Arca and forced off with medial knee ligament damage. The injury meant he missed the remaining three games of the season – although he was able to make a cameo appearance in a farewell testimonial at Gallowgate against Celtic. Shearer appeared for kick-off before leaving the field, returning in the final seconds to sign off by converting a penalty with typical aplomb.

Proceeds from the sell-out game, merchandising and other events eventually totalled £1.64 million – which was donated to various charitable causes.

Joining BBC TV as a regular panellist on *Match of The Day*, Shearer began working towards his coaching qualifications only to then find himself making an unexpected return to St James' Park in April 2008.

In a last desperate attempt to avoid relegation from the top flight, Newcastle United approached their former number-nine hero to take control of the side for the final eight games of the season.

Sadly for him and the Magpies, he and assistant Iain Dowie were only able to guide the black and whites to one victory and two draws and relegation was confirmed on the final day of the season with a single-goal loss at Martin O'Neill's Aston Villa.

Widely expected to be appointed manager on a permanent basis, an apparent communication breakdown between the two parties resulted in Shearer returning to his punditry and Chris Hughton taking over once more at Gallowgate.

Alan Shearer factfile
Born: Gosforth, August 13th 1970
Newcastle career: 404 apps, 206 goals (1996–2006)
Other clubs: Southampton, Blackburn Rovers
International: England, 63 caps, 30 goals

— TWELFTH NIGHT —

- Albert Bennett holds the distinction of being the first ever Newcastle United substitute, following a change in the rules at the start of the 1965/66 season allowing teams to name a twelfth man (although the sub was only allowed to come onto the pitch to replace an injured player). Consequently, Bennett remained firmly seated on the bench during the Magpies' 2–2 draw with Nottingham Forest at St James' Park on August 21st 1965.

- The honour of being Newcastle's first playing sub went to Ollie Burton on September 4th 1965 when he replaced Trevor Hockey (who had sustained a shin injury) during a 2–0 home victory over Northampton Town. And it was Burton who became the first Newcastle player to net after coming on to the field as a substitute, scoring in a 1–2 defeat to Lincoln City at Sincil Bank in the Football League Cup on September 13th 1967.

- On August 29th 1987 the number of substitutes permissible was raised to two, with the Magpies first using their number 12 and 14 in a 0–1 home loss to Nottingham Forest. On that occasion Kenny Wharton and Paul Goddard gave way to John Anderson and Andy Thomas.

- Three substitutes were permitted for the first time at the start of the 1995/96 season, with then-manager Kevin Keegan making a trio of replacements for the first time in the sixth Premiership game of the season, the visit of Manchester City to Tyneside. In a 3–1 victory for United on September 16th 1995, Warren Barton gave way to Steve Watson, Scott Sellars replaced John Beresford and Ruel Fox was introduced for Peter Beardsley.

- The first-ever substitute to appear back in the 1965/66 season was Keith Peacock of Charlton Athletic. His son Gavin later played for Newcastle United.

— #9 DREAM PART I —

Although the so-called 'Summer of Love' didn't really have much of an impact on Tyneside, Newcastle fans can still claim a (slightly tenuous) link to the record that what was for many the soundtrack of the psychedelic era.

On June 1st 1967 The Beatles released *Sgt Pepper's Lonely Hearts Club Band* on the Parlophone label – an album routinely cited as one of the most innovative and inspirational pieces of popular music ever recorded.

As well as the ground-breaking material though, much attention was also focused on the cover artwork, which consisted of the 'Fab Four' plus a montage of more than 70 iconic personalities that The Beatles themselves had chosen.

These appeared in life-size cardboard cut-out form – a concept originally devised by Paul McCartney, designed by Peter Blake, created by art director Robert Fraser and photographed on March 30th 1967 by Michael Cooper.

Included among the various world leaders, entertainers, philoso-phers and poets were three sportsmen – boxer Sonny Liston, Olympic swimmer Johnny Weissmuller and former Liverpool centre forward Albert Stubbins (Everton legend William Ralph 'Dixie' Dean was also considered but not included).

Born in Wallsend, Stubbins had moved to Liverpool from Newcastle in 1946, rapidly becoming a Kop favourite and playing for the Anfield club until 1953. His place in the montage has variously been claimed to have been at the urging of both John Lennon and Paul McCartney, the former allegedly because Stubbins was a great favourite of his father Fred Lennon. McCartney also seems to have been a Stubbins fan, later sending him a telegram: "Well done Albert for all those glorious years in football. Long may you bob and weave."

Regardless of whose choice it was, a photo of a grinning Albert in his Liverpool strip can be seen towards the centre of the group – just behind Marlene Dietrich.

In 2003, the International Federation of the Phonographic Industry (IFPI), certified that worldwide sales of *Sgt Pepper's* . . . had exceeded 32 million – that's an awful lot of Alberts . . .

— FAMILIAR FACES —

The top twenty competitive appearance makers for the club are:

Rank	Player	Total	Timespan
1	Jimmy Lawrence	496	1904–1922
2	Frank Hudspeth	472	1910–1929
3	Shay Given	463	1997–2009
4	Frank Clark	457	1962–1975
5	Bill McCracken	432	1904–1923
6	Alf McMichael	431	1949–1963
7	David Craig	412	1962–1978
8	Bobby Mitchell	408	1949–1961
9	Alan Shearer	404	1996–2006
10	Jackie Milburn	397	1946–1957
11	Robert Lee	380	1992–2002
12	Wilf Low	367	1909–1924
12	Tom McDonald	367	1921–1931
13	Iam McFaul	355	1966–1975
14	Andy Aitken	349	1895–1906
15	Frank Brennan	347	1946–1956
16	Bob Moncur	345	1960–1974
17	Jackie Rutherford	334	1902–1913

18	Shola Ameobi	333	2000–present
19	John Anderson	332	1982–1992
20	Bobby Cowell	327	1943–1956
20	Kenny Wharton	327	1978–1989

— NEWCASTLE LEGENDS: PETER BEARDSLEY —

Time fails to dim the brilliance of Peter Beardsley's finishing

Spotted playing youth football on Tyneside, Peter Beardsley had trials at Gillingham, Cambridge United, Burnley and Newcastle United without earning a professional contract. For a while it seemed the talented but lightweight schemer would have to consider a career outside football.

Fortunately for Beardsley, former Magpies captain Bob Moncur got wind of his abilities and talked the 18-year-old into playing for his Carlisle United reserve side at Newcastle Blue Star in 1979. Beardsley scored that night in a 3–2 win at the Wheatsheaf and quickly agreed terms with the Brunton Park club, where he continued to earn rave reviews.

In 1981 he moved to the North American Soccer League with Vancouver Whitecaps but two years later joined Arthur Cox's Newcastle side after a brief one-game flirtation with Manchester United.

Beardsley helped Newcastle to promotion in his first season with the club but after Cox was replaced by Jack Charlton, he found himself competing for a place up front with burly forwards Tony Cunningham and George Reilly. Under new manager Willie McFaul, Beardsley was back in favour, but he grew increasingly frustrated with a perceived lack of ambition at the club.

In July 1987 he departed for Liverpool in a record £1.9 million deal, and remained on Merseyside for a six-year spell which included two seasons at Everton. It was during this period that Beardsley won the bulk of his 59 England caps, forming a successful forward partnership with Gary Lineker.

In 1993, Kevin Keegan brought Beardsley, now aged 32, back to Tyneside. Using his exceptional close ball skills to supply the prolific Andy Cole when he wasn't scoring sensational goals himself, he was a prime mover in establishing Newcastle United back in the top flight.

After leaving Newcastle for a second time in 1997, he took in stops at Bolton Wanderers, Manchester City, Fulham, Hartlepool and Doncaster Rovers.

A sell-out testimonial game at St James' Park in 1999 saw his boyhood favourites Celtic come to town, the occasion featuring the likes of Kenny Dalglish, Andy Cole and Kevin Keegan back in black and white for one night. None of these stars were surprised to learn that Beardsley, one of the most enthusiastic footballers of his generation, had played for Hartlepool's first team the evening before his big night.

For those who saw this skilful, creative and clever player at his peak certain memories are embedded. Among the most vivid moments are the chip over Brighton goalkeeper Joe Corrigan on the final day of the 1983/84 season, a New Years' Day hat-trick at home to Sunderland in 1985, and from his second spell, superb late winners at White Hart Lane and Selhurst Park. Time fails to dim the brilliance of his finishing.

Returning to United for the third time in 1999, Beardsley has held various coaching posts with the club's Academy and Reserve squads and also served the club in a PR capacity.

Peter Beardsley factfile
Born: Longbenton, January 18th 1961
Newcastle career: 324 apps, 119 goals (1983–87 and 1993–97)
Other clubs: Carlisle United, Vancouver Whitecaps, Manchester United, Liverpool, Bolton Wanderers, Manchester City (loan), Fulham, Hartlepool United, Doncaster Rovers, Melbourne Knights
International: England, 59 caps, 9 goals

— SHEARER STATS —

Some number-crunching in honour of Newcastle United's record goal-scorer:

Shearer's overall league record:
Alan Shearer career record (Premiership/Div1): 558 games, 283 goals
Alan Shearer career record (all comps): 733 games, 379 goals

By club:

Southampton	140 starts (18 as substitute)	43 goals
Blackburn Rovers	165 starts (6 as substitute)	130 goals
Newcastle United	395 starts (9 as substitute)	206 goals

By season:

Season Club	Games (League)	(all)	Goals (League)	(all)
1987/88 Southampton	5	5	3	3
1988/89 Southampton	10	10	0	0
1989/90 Southampton	26	35	3	5
1990/91 Southampton	36	48	4	14
1991/92 Southampton	41	60	13	21
1992/93 Blackburn Rovers	21	26	16	22
1993/94 Blackburn Rovers	40	48	31	34
1994/95 Blackburn Rovers	42	49	34	37
1995/96 Blackburn Rovers	35	48	31	37
1996/97 Newcastle United	31	40	25	28
1997/98 Newcastle United	17	23	2	7
1998/99 Newcastle United	30	40	14	21
1999/00 Newcastle United	37	50	23	30

2000/01 Newcastle United	19	23	5	7
2001/02 Newcastle United	37	46	23	27
2002/03 Newcastle United	35	48	17	25
2003/04 Newcastle United	37	51	22	28
2004/05 Newcastle United	28	42	7	19
2005/06 Newcastle United	32	41	10	14

Note: Alan Shearer's 63 full England caps and 30 goals are not included in these figures.

— THE INTERNATIONAL BRIGADE —

The evening of February 29th 2012 saw two former Newcastle players make their international managerial debut – while the tragically curtailed life of a third was celebrated.

At Wembley Stadium, Stuart Pearce took charge of England on a caretaker basis following the abrupt departure of Fabio Capello, Holland defeating the Three Lions 3–2 in a friendly encounter. In Belfast, meanwhile, Michael O'Neill got off to a losing start as the permanent Northern Ireland boss, as his new charges lost 0–3 to Norway at Windsor Park.

A more sombre occasion took place at the Cardiff City Stadium, however, as Wales met Costa Rica in a memorial game for the late Gary Speed – who was in the Wales manager's post when found dead at his home in November 2011.

Other former Newcastle players who have managed internationally include:

John Barnes (Jamaica)
Jack Carr (Denmark)
Jesse Carver (Netherlands)
Joe Devine (Iceland)
Kevin Keegan (England)
Temuri Ketsbaia (Georgia)
Iam McFaul (Guam)
Liam Tuohy (Ireland)
Peter Withe (Thailand, Indonesia)
Ray Wood (Cyprus, Kenya)

And a handful of ex-Magpie coaches and managers have also managed internationally:

Tommy Burns (Scotland) (caretaker)
Jack Charlton (Ireland)
Joe Kinnear (India, Nepal)
Duggie Livingstone (Belgium, Ireland)
Bobby Robson (England)
Mick Wadsworth (Democratic Republic of Congo)

— THE NAME NOW LEAVING
FROM PLATFORM NINE —

The name of Newcastle United once adorned the sides of a railway locomotive – but only the most keen-eyed would ever have seen it for themselves thanks to some apparent skulduggery on the part of the London and North Eastern Railway.

Often referred to as the 'Footballer Class', the B17 class of locomotives were designed by Sir Herbert Nigel Gresley, with 73 built at various locations between 1928 and 1937; 25 of which were given the names of English football clubs.

No. 2858 rolled out of Darlington Works on May 28th 1936 resplendent in green livery and with a nameplate incorporating a brass football, black and white decoration and the name 'Newcastle United'.

However, when the locomotive appeared at a railway exhibition in Romford just ten days later, it bore nameplates proclaiming it to be 'The Essex Regiment' – a name it carried until it was withdrawn from operating service and scrapped in December 1959.

The reasons for the change of heart were never fully explained, although club rivalries may have played some part in the decision. In the event, the B17 class were never a common sight in the North East due to a lack of power.

It's presumed that the 'Newcastle United' nameplates were scrapped as they have never surfaced, but a replica nameplate was commissioned and presented to the club in 2003 by Magpies fan and railway enthusiast David Tyreman.

— 'THE PIRATE' —

Newcastle chairman between 1964 and 1978, Lord Westwood remains a controversial figure despite passing away in 1991.

Much of the blame for the stagnation of the club in the 1970s and a lack of investment in the team and stadium is laid at his door by commentators of the era. Westwood, who was popularly known as 'The Pirate' due to an eye patch that covered his right eye (the result of a car accident), resigned as chairman in 1978 and left the Board altogether in 1981 – refusing on both occasions to use his own funds to underwrite financial rescue packages.

A one-time president of the Football League, it was said of Westwood that he would swap his patch to cover his good eye when watching Newcastle lose.

— FANZINES —

August 1988 saw the publication of the first issue of *The Mag* – an unofficial fanzine composed and compiled by a small group of Newcastle fans and billing itself as an independent supporters' magazine

Priced at 50p and with a cover including a photograph of a young and trendily attired Paul Gascoigne, *The Mag* certainly wasn't short of targets to snipe at.

Issues covered in this debut copy included the enduring racist chanting at St James' Park and the unwelcome presence of National Front supporters selling their racist publication *Bulldog* outside the ground on matchdays.

Also the subject of grumbling was the continued lack of covered standing accommodation at the stadium, which at the time still had two open ends.

The threat from proposed new coverage of games on satellite TV was also mentioned, while the departure of Peter Beardsley earlier in the year to Liverpool – allegedly to fund the cost of constructing the Milburn Stand – was also discussed.

Fast forward to the end of the 2011/12 season and *The Mag* has enjoyed an uninterrupted run, reaching issue number 268.

A sister publication *True Faith* first appeared at the start of the 1999/00 season, taking a more left-field look at Toon-related events and providing a platform for those writing about football culture. By mid 2012, it had reached issue 95.

Various other unofficial Newcastle United fanzines have come and gone over the years, including:

Black and White
The Geordie Times
The Giant Awakes
Half Mag Half Biscuit
Jim's Bald Heid
The Mighty Quinn
The Number Nine
Oh Wi Ye Naa
Once Upon A Tyne
Talk of the Toon
Talk of the Tyne
Toon Army News
Black and White Daft
Toon Talk

— CHALKED OFF? —

Newcastle United were involved in one of the most controversial incidents in the history of the FA Cup, when they faced Arsenal at Wembley in the 1932 final.

Arsenal took the lead in the 12th minute, but Newcastle equalised seven minutes before half-time with what *The Times* described as 'the most controversial goal in English football history'.

Chasing a ball down the line, Newcastle's Jimmy Richardson stretched to reach the ball and delivered a cross into Jack Allen to score. However, many in the stadium felt the ball had crossed the line before Richardson crossed it.

Allen struck again on 72 minutes to give his side the win and the distinction of being the first side ever to have come from behind to win a Wembley FA Cup final.

However some discontent among supporters and Arsenal officials was evident, with claims that the ball had gone out of play before the first goal strengthened by newspaper reports of the game and photographs which appeared to back up the claims. The incident even knocked Adolf Hitler's victory in the Prussian elections off the front page.

And the conviction that there had been a miscarriage grew the following week when British Movietone News footage of the goal was shown in cinemas that purported to show that the ball was out of play via primitive freeze frame technology.

Invoking the spirit of future Gunners boss Arsene Wenger, Newcastle goalscorer Jack Allen told *The Guardian* newspaper: "From my position I could not see whether it had gone out of play or not."

While Richardson similarly claimed: "I was concentrating so hard on reaching the ball that I couldn't tell you whether it was over the line or not."

Match referee Percy Harper remained adamant, however: "I gave the goal in accordance with the rules and regulations of the Football Association – it was definitely a goal. The ball was definitely in play. I was so certain that the goal was good that I did not even consider it necessary to consult the linesman, and I am still just as certain. I was, of course, well up with the play, and was in a position to see the incident clearly. Whatever the film may appear to show will not make me alter my opinion."

— TRICKSTERS —

By the end of the 2011/12 season, nine Newcastle players had scored three goals or more at least once in a single Premier League fixture for the club as follows:

1993/94	Peter Beardsley v Wimbledon (h)	35 minutes
1993/94	Andy Cole v Liverpool (h)	26 minutes
1993/94	Andy Cole v Coventry City (h)	28 minutes
1995/96	Les Ferdinand v Wimbledon (h)	28 minutes
1996/97	Alan Shearer v Leicester City (h)	13 minutes
1999/00	Alan Shearer v Sheffield Wednesday (h)	12 minutes
2005/06	Michael Owen v West Ham United (a)	85 minutes
2010/11	Andy Carroll v Aston Villa (h)	59 minutes
2010/11	Kevin Nolan v Sunderland (h)	49 minutes
2010/11	Leon Best v West Ham United (h)	42 minutes
2011/12	Demba Ba v Blackburn Rovers (h)	27 minutes
2011/12	Demba Ba v Stoke City (a)	69 minutes

(Alan Shearer went on to score five against the Owls in 1999)

— CROWDED HOUSE —

January 2008 saw Newcastle incur their heaviest Premier League defeat in front of the biggest live audience to watch them in the competition when caretaker boss Nigel Pearson took the Magpies to Old Trafford.

Stonewalling the home side for the opening 45 minutes, a 0–0 scoreline at half-time soon began to alter, though, with Cristiano Ronaldo helping himself to a hat-trick and Shay Given also picking a Carlos Tevez brace and one from Rio Ferdinand out of his net. Future Magpie Danny Simpson, meanwhile, appeared as a second-half substitute for the Red Devil.

The largest crowds attending Newcastle games during each season of their Premier League participation have been:

1993/94	44,601	Liverpool (Anfield)
1994/95	43,795	Manchester United (Old Trafford)
1995/96	42,024	Manchester United (Old Trafford)
1996/97	55,236	Manchester United (Old Trafford)
1997/98	55,194	Manchester United (Old Trafford)
1998/99	55,174	Manchester United (Old Trafford)
1999/00	55,190	Manchester United (Old Trafford)
2000/01	67,477	Manchester United (Old Trafford)
2001/02	67,646	Manchester United (Old Trafford)
2002/03	67,619	Manchester United (Old Trafford)
2003/04	67,622	Manchester United (Old Trafford)
2004/05	67,845	Manchester United (Old Trafford)
2005/06	67,858	Manchester United (Old Trafford)
2006/07	75,664	Manchester United (Old Trafford)
2007/08	75,965	Manchester United (Old Trafford)
2008/09	75,512	Manchester United (Old Trafford)
2010/11	75,221	Manchester United (Old Trafford)
2011/12	75,594	Manchester United (Old Trafford)

— AND HERE'S TO BOBBY MONCUR —

It's a well-worn path to the banks of the Danube, striped goalposts and a funny shaped cup, but Newcastle's Fairs Cup success of 1968/69 remains the last bona fide trophy that the Magpies have won.

Beginning with a resounding home victory on the Magpies'

European debut, five two-legged ties brought the club to a home and away final games against Hungarian side Ujpesti Dozsa:

Route to Glory:

Opponent	Score	Newcastle scorer(s)	Crowd
Feyenoord (h)	4–0	Scott, Robson, Gibb, Davies	46,348
Feyenoord (a)	0–2		45,000
Sporting Lisbon (a)	1–1	Scott	9,000
Sporting Lisbon (h)	1–0	Robson	53,747
Real Zaragoza (a)	2–3	Davies, Robson	22,000
Real Zaragoza (h)	2–1	Robson, Gibb	56,055
Vitoria Setubal (h)	5–1	Foggon, Robson, Davies, Robson, Gibb	57,662
Vitoria Setubal (a)	1–3	Davies	34,000
Rangers (a)	0–0		75,580
Rangers (h)	2–0	Scott, Sinclair	59,303
Ujpesti Dozsa (h)	3–0	Moncur 2, Scott	59,234
Ujpesti Dozsa (a)	3–2	Moncur, Arentoft, Foggon	34,000

Final line-ups:

May 29th 1969 St James' Park, Newcastle:
McFaul, Craig, Burton, Moncur, Clark, Gibb, Arentoft, Scott, Davies, Robson, Sinclair (Foggon) Substitutes unused: Hope, Craggs
Goal times: Moncur 63, 71, Scott 84

June 11th 1969 Megyeri Stadium, Budapest:
McFaul, Craig, Burton, Moncur, Clark, Gibb, Arentoft, Scott (Foggon), Davies, Robson, Sinclair. Substitutes unused: Hope, McNamee
Goal times: Moncur 46, Arentoft 53, Foggon 68 (For Ujpesti: Bene 30, Gorocs 43)

Across the 12 ties, Newcastle named 25 players, of whom four were on the field for every minute: Willie McFaul, Tommy Gibb, Wyn Davies and 'Pop' Robson. A further two – Frank Clark and Jimmy Scott – appeared in all 12 ties at some stage. The other 16 players utilised were: Geoff Allen, Benny Arentoft, Albert Bennett, Ollie Burton, John Craggs, David Craig, Keith Dyson, Dave Elliott, Alan Foggon, Ron Guthrie, Arthur Horsfield, Jim Iley, John McNamee, Bobby Moncur, Jackie Sinclair and Graham Winstanley. Non-appearing goalkeeping substitutes Gordon Marshall, John Hope and Dave Clarke completed the squad.

— FOR FORK'S SAKE —

Having ended their four-year winless run in London at the 30th time of asking, Newcastle's players were entitled to feel pleased with themselves on December 19th 2001.

An eventful 3–1 win against Arsenal at Highbury had propelled Newcastle to the top of the Premiership. Unbeknown to them however, a higher power had been at work.

In the following day's *Evening Chronicle* cutlery-bending psychic Uri Geller described how he led the Spoon Army for one night:

> "I knew the team would win. I am so happy for everyone who supports them. It was exactly what I said.
>
> "I arrived late and had no ticket. But the moment I got out of the car and touched the Highbury stadium, the Arsenal player Ray Parlour was sent off.
>
> "I started screaming and shouting for Newcastle to win. And soon after the start of the second half I said to my friend that Shearer would score from a penalty. That was half an hour before it happened. But I knew it. I knew the team would win. I am so happy for everyone who supports them. It was exactly what I said.
>
> "While Newcastle were scoring their winning goals I was running round the outside of the ground 11 times to lift the hoodoo.
>
> "I even predicted the 3–1 scoreline after I got to the ground. I sat in the car and listened to the game on the radio. And after Arsenal scored I decided it was time to act.
>
> "There was a lot to do with the number 11. Newcastle had not won in 29 games and two plus nine is 11. Number 11 is very mystical and powerful. So I ran around the ground 11 times. The facts speak for themselves.
>
> "I hope Newcastle will win the league but I have to concentrate and see. Right now I have done what you wanted.
>
> "It is almost a guarantee the team will win when I have a moment to talk to the players in the dressing room, I wasn't able to do that last night but I was physically close to them which is important."

Despite Uri's powers, Newcastle failed to win the Premiership that season, ultimately finishing back in fourth, some 16 points behind champions Arsenal. And things got worse for Geller, with the Exeter City co-chairman seeing his "beloved" Grecians relegated into the

Football Conference in 2003 – despite bringing his pal Michael Jackson to visit their St James' Park ground.

— EDSON ENCOUNTER —

The end of the 1971/72 season saw Newcastle embark on an Asian tour, which included visits to Thailand, Hong Kong and Iran.

Providing the opposition in Hong Kong were the Brazilian side Santos, whose most famous player Edson Arantes do Nascimento (aka Pele) was in their line-up.

Newcastle led 2–1 at the interval thanks to a long-range effort from Tony Green and a John Tudor header – Pele at this stage having been virtually anonymous.

However, that all changed in the second half as Pele set to work, scoring a hat-trick in a devastating 15-minute spell that enthralled those fans present and ensured that Newcastle lost 2–4.

John Tudor recalled: "The delicate close-control skills, the amazing acceleration, the powerhouse shooting had the crowd in ecstasy. It was like trying to stop a flash of lightning."

His job done, Pele then left the field – pausing only to shake hands with the stunned Newcastle players.

— DREAM STARTS PART I —

Newcastle United players who scored a hat-trick or better on their competitive debut for the Magpies:

Year	Player	Opponent/venue	
1946	Len Shackleton	Newport County (h)	6 goals
1989	Mick Quinn	Leeds United (h)	4 goals
1926	Bob McKay	West Bromwich Albion (h)	3 goals
1935	Wilf Bott	Bury (h)	3 goals

Shackleton's debut came in an amazing 13–0 success in which his new team-mate Charlie Wayman (who scored four in the game) missed a penalty in the opening moments.

Coming in the days before television coverage and the FA's Dubious Goals Committee, 'Shack' was credited with his sixth and Newcastle's 13th, although Newport's Ken Wookey may have got the final touch. What isn't in doubt, however, is his incredible scoring rate, as he notched his second, third and fourth goals in this game within a 155-second period.

— IS THIS THE WAY TO . . . ? —

Current Football League stadia that Newcastle have never visited competitively:

AFC Wimbledon (Kingsmeadow)*
Aldershot Town (Recreation Ground)*
Barnet (Underhill Stadium)*
Bristol Rovers (Memorial Stadium)*
Burton Albion (Pirelli Stadium)*
Chesterfield (B2NET Stadium)
Colchester United (Weston Homes Community Stadium)*
Crawley Town (Broadfield Stadium)*
Dagenham & Redbridge (Victoria Road)*
Hartlepool United (Victoria Park)
Macclesfield Town (Moss Rose)*
Millwall (New Den)*
Milton Keynes Dons (Stadium:mk)*
Morecambe (Globe Arena)*
Northampton Town (Sixfields Stadium)*
Oxford United (Kassam Stadium)*
Rochdale (Spotland)
Shrewsbury Town (New Meadow)*
Torquay United (Plainmoor)
Walsall (Bescot Stadium)
Wycombe Wanderers (Adams Park)*
Yeovil Town (Huish Park)

*Stadia yet to be visited at any level of football e.g. friendlies, reserves etc.

— NEWCASTLE'S TOP LEAGUE CUP SCORERS —

Player	Total
Malcolm Macdonald	12
Andy Cole	8
Shola Ameobi	7
Alan Gowling	7
Alan Shearer	7
Gavin Peacock	5
Peter Beardsley	4
Craig Bellamy	4
Micky Burns	4
Paul Cannell	4
Peter Lovenkrands	4

— OUT OF AFRICA —

The 2012 staging of the African Cup of Nations saw Newcastle manager Alan Pardew forced to select his side without a trio of players, as Cheick Tiote, Demba Ba and new signing Papiss Demba Cisse all received international call-ups.

To date, 11 current and former/future players have played in the mid-season event, for five different countries:

Cameroon: Having played at each event since 1998, Geremi's first season at St James' Park saw him feature at his sixth tournament in 2008, in Ghana. Unlike 2000 and 2002 though, he finished on the losing side in the final.

By the time of his seventh appearance in 2010, Geremi was a Magpie in name only, joining Turkish side Ankaragucu at the conclusion of the Finals, in Angola. Cameroon's failure to qualify for the 2012 event then brought his run to an end.

Democratic Republic of Congo: The first call-up of a current Magpie player came in 2002, when Lomana LuaLua joined his fellow countrymen in Mali for a campaign that ended at the quarter-final stage without him getting on the scoresheet.

By 2004, LuaLua was the DR Congo captain (appointed by ex-Magpie coach Mick Wadsworth). However, three straight losses saw them eliminated from the Finals in Tunisia, LuaLua again failing to score but picking up a red card. That duck was finally broken with a goal against Togo in 2006, but DR Congo exited from the tournament in Egypt at the quarter-final stage.

Ivory Coast: Featuring in 2010, Cheick Tiote returned for the 2012 event (staged jointly in Gabon and Equatorial Guinea) and played his part as the Elephants cruised through to the Finals. After 120 minutes failed to produce a goal against Zambia in the Gabonese City of Libreville though, the game went to penalties. Cheick netted his, but Zambia won 8–7.

Nigeria: Celestine Babayaro appeared in both the 2000 and 2002 Finals while a Chelsea player, while Obafemi Martins was a Magpie at the 2008 event. He had joined Germans Wolfsburg by 2010, when he netted his first goal, against Mozambique.

Senegal: The Lions of Teranaga relied upon the services of Magpies defenders Habib Beye and Abdoulaye Faye at the 2008 Finals in Ghana, along with Lamine Diatta – who moved to United shortly afterwards. That trio had also seen service in both 2004 and 2006, while Diatta and Beye appeared at the 2002 Finals. Defensive midfielder Amdy Faye, meanwhile, featured in both 2002 and 2006, the latter when a Newcastle player.

The 2012 event then showcased United's new strike partnership of Cisse and Ba, but they were soon free to begin their playing partnership at club level after failing to find the net as bookie's favourites Senegal lost all three group games.

— UPPERS AND DOWNERS —

Since Newcastle United first took their place in Division Two for the 1893/94 season, the club has enjoyed – and endured – no fewer than 11 movements between the top two divisions in England.

Season	Move	Movers
1897/98	Promoted	Burnley, **Newcastle**
	Relegated	None
1933/34	Relegated	**Newcastle**, Sheffield United
	Promoted	Grimsby Town, Preston North End
1947/48	Promoted	Birmingham City, **Newcastle**
	Relegated	Blackburn Rovers, Grimsby Town
1960/61	Relegated	**Newcastle**, Preston North End
	Promoted	Ipswich Town, Sheffield United

1964/65	Promoted	**Newcastle**, Northampton Town
	Relegated	Wolverhampton Wanderers, Birmingham City
1977/78	Relegated	West Ham United, **Newcastle**, Leicester City
	Promoted	Bolton Wanderers, Southampton, Tottenham Hotspur
1983/84	Promoted	Chelsea, Sheffield Wednesday, **Newcastle**
	Relegated	Birmingham City, Notts County, Wolverhampton Wanderers
1988/89	Relegated	Middlesbrough, West Ham United, **Newcastle**
	Promoted	Chelsea, Manchester City, Crystal Palace*
1992/93	Promoted	**Newcastle**, West Ham United, Swindon Town*
	Relegated	Crystal Palace, Middlesbrough, Nottingham Forest
2008/09	Relegated	**Newcastle**, Middlesbrough, West Bromwich Albion
	Promoted	Wolverhampton Wanderers, Birmingham City, Burnley*
2009/10	Promoted	Newcastle, West Bromwich Albion, Blackpool*
	Relegated	Burnley, Hull City, Portsmouth

(*promoted via the playoffs)

From 1897/98 to 1988/89, all of the above saw Newcastle move between Football League Divisions One and Two. 1992/93 was from the renamed Division One to The Premier League and both 2008/09 and 2009/10 involved the Premier League and The Championship.

— TREBLE CHANCE —

Hat-trick pioneers for the club:

First in Division Two: Willie Thompson in a 6–0 home win over Woolwich Arsenal on September 30th 1893.

First in Division One: Jock Peddie in an 8–0 home win over Notts

County on October 26th 1901.

First in FA Cup: Bill Appleyard in a 5–1 home win over Grimsby Town on March 7th 1908.

First in Anglo-Italian Cup: Malcolm Macdonald in a 5–1 home win over Crystal Palace on May 21st 1973.

First in League Cup: Malcolm Macdonald in a 6–0 home win over Doncaster Rovers on October 8th 1973.

First in Premiership: Peter Beardsley in a 4–0 home win over Wimbledon on October 30th 1993.

First in UEFA Cup: Robert Lee in a 5–0 away win over Royal Antwerp on September 13th 1994.

First in Champions League: Faustino Asprilla in a 3–2 home win over Barcelona on September 17th 1997.

— MEMORY MATCHES 3 —

Oct 1st 1991

Tranmere Rovers 1 Newcastle United 1 (Zenith Data Systems Cup)

Barely a month after losing 2–3 on the same ground in a Division Two fixture, United were back at Prenton Park for a minor cup competition previously christened the Full Members Cup. Manager Ossie Ardiles selected a full-strength lineup for the tie, which was watched by less than half of the 11,000 crowd present for the previous game but televised live across the UK via the-then fledgling broadcaster that came to be Sky Television.

Ahead through a deflected Lee Clark shot, Rovers levelled through McNab before John Aldridge seized on Robbie Elliott's poor back pass and dinked home his first goal of the night. The United left back soon atoned for his error though, finding Gavin Peacock down the left flank and his centre reached Mick Quinn, whose shot was parried by 'keeper Eric Nixon – only for Andy Hunt to knock in.

With the scores level on 2–2 at the break, Newcastle then regained the lead through a well-taken Gavin Peacock effort – only to be pegged back when Steele beat Srnicek to leave the scores tied at 90 minutes and the tie moving on to 30 minutes additional time.

A suicidal back pass from Kevin Scott then left Pav stranded and presented Aldridge with an empty net to walk the ball into and further slack defending allowed Martindale in seconds later to put Rovers 5–3 up in the first period of added time. However, Lee Clark then netted before the interval, before setting up Peacock for a point blank finish. And when Alan Neilson was fouled in the area and Quinn netted the penalty in the final moments of added time, Newcastle looked to have pulled off a sensational 6–5 success.

There was still time for Rovers though to counter-attack and Aldridge to crumble in the box when pushed by Hunt, getting up to make it 6–6 and complete his hat trick with a stop-start penalty conversion that left the tie to be decided on a penalty shootout.

A long-standing weakness at such things was soon continuing with Quinn hitting a post and Clark having his effort saved, between which Irons converted. After Malkin scored, substitute David Roche did pull one back before Hughes made it 3–1 and left Rovers on the brink. Gavin Peacock kept his side in it, before Srnicek finally got near one and dived full-length to deny Higgins. However future Rover Liam O'Brien was then denied by Nixon to send Tranmere through 3–2.

NUFC: Srnicek, Neilson, Elliott, O'Brien, Scott, Bradshaw, Clark, Peacock, Quinn, Hunt, Brock (Roche)

— BREWERS DROOP —

On 15th April 1895 Newcastle played the final game of their second season in Division Two, with a tenth place finish assured. However, their away fixture against Burton Wanderers was to prove memorable for all the wrong reasons, as their Derby Turn ground proved to be venue for United's record defeat.

Trailing 0–4 at half time, the final score was 0–9 in favour of the home side, who avenged their 6–3 defeat on Tyneside earlier that season. For a team who had only managed four clean sheets in their previous 31 league and cup games that season, conceding goals wasn't a major shock to Newcastle and their porous defence.

The rigours of playing two home games in the three days running up to the Wanderers game may be a partial excuse. However, the following season saw all but two of the Newcastle side who appeared in the record defeat shipped out.

Some 38 years later, the Magpies 'celebrated' the anniversary of their record loss by slipping to a mere 1–6 defeat away to Leeds United.

— FAMILIAR FOES —

Since the two sides first met home and away within a few weeks of each other in September 1893 in Division Two, Newcastle United's most frequent competitive opponents have been Arsenal (known as 'Woolwich Arsenal' until 1914).

While St James' Park has remained the home venue for the Magpies throughout, Arsenal have moved twice since hosting Newcastle for the first time at their Manor Ground in Plumstead. A move across the Thames came in 1913, with Newcastle's debut at Highbury in August 1919 marked by a 1–0 away win. November 2006 then saw the Magpies visit the Emirates Stadium for the first time, a 1–1 draw being the outcome.

Newcastle's top ten most played opponents:

Opponent	P	W	D	L	F	A
Arsenal	163	65	36	62	228	228
Manchester City	159	70	37	52	241	215
Liverpool	157	45	38	74	193	267
Everton	154	62	32	60	232	226
Aston Villa	147	63	31	53	231	236
Manchester United	146	39	34	73	216	283
Chelsea	143	47	36	60	179	212
Tottenham Hotspur	139	52	30	57	209	218
Sunderland	139	51	45	43	210	205
Blackburn	133	55	29	49	202	195

— TYNE NINE IDOLS —

Papiss Demba Cisse twice came the width of a goal frame away from joining a select club of Newcastle United players in a game against Wigan Athletic in April 2012.

The Senegal-born striker came into the game having scored in each of his previous six appearances for the club, but saw the run end as he couldn't find the net in a 0–4 loss to the Latics.

Only three of Cisse's predecessors had netted in seven consecutive league fixtures: Len White in both 1958 and 1961, Paul Goddard in 1987 and Alan Shearer in 1996 – the latter scoring in five games, missing three through injury and then returning a month later to rack up his sixth and seventh.

The club's all-time consecutive scoring record remains nine league and cup games, a feat only ever managed by Willie Wardrope way back in 1895, when he netted a total of 13 times in that run.

A century later, Les Ferdinand came close to emulating that when converting 12 goals across eight successive games – only to come agonisingly close to scoring in the ninth, at Spurs.

— MEMORY MATCHES 4 —

19th September 1999

Newcastle United 8 Sheffield Wednesday 0 (Premier League)

Ruud Gullit's departure from St James' Park less than a month after the start of the 1999/2000 campaign left Tyneside breathing a collective sigh of relief and after away games against Chelsea and CSKA Sofia, the incoming Bobby Robson made his Gallowgate debut against the Owls.

The first ten minutes gave little hint of what was to come, before Kieron Dyer set up Aaron Hughes to head in his first goal for the club – Robson having selected the defender after opting not to bring in veteran centre half Colin Hendry to bolster his backline.

It took until the half hour though for a further breakthrough, when Dyer again centred and Alan Shearer flicked home his first goal from open play that season. Shearer then made it 3–0 shortly after from the penalty spot after referee Neale Barry spotted a handball and the number nine completed a sensational 12-minute treble when stealing ahead of Des Walker to convert another Dyer cross.

Bucking the trend of high-scoring first halves, the second 45 instantly unfolded in similar fashion, as Danny Wilson's demoralised Wednesday saw Dyer stoop to head home seconds after the restart. A temporary lull then ended with a fine Gary Speed header on 78 minutes before Shearer gobbled up his fourth and United's seventh after a defensive lapse. With six minutes to play substitute Paul Robinson tumbled over in the box and looked set to take the resultant spot kick – before the number nine arrived and claimed the ball before blasting past the luckless Kevin Pressman to make it 8–0 – the first time United had reached that total on home soil in nearly 40 years. Watching from the Owl's bench – and doubtless glad not to be called upon was Magpies old boy, Pavel Srnicek.

NUFC: Harper, Barton, Goma, Hughes, Domi (Glass), Lee, Solano, Dyer (Robinson), Shearer, Ketsbaia (McClen), Speed.

— AWAY THE LADS —

Aside from St James' Park, the venue at which Newcastle have earned the most Premiership points is Villa Park. Here's the complete record of how and where the Magpies' have earned their points on the road since promotion in 1993.

Opposition	Frequency	Record	Pts
Aston Villa	15 visits	6 wins, 5 draws, 4 defeats	23
Middlesbrough	12 visits	6 wins, 4 draws, 2 defeats	22
Leeds United	11 visits	6 wins, 3 draws, 2 defeats	21
Tottenham Hotspur	15 visits	6 wins, 1 draw, 8 defeats	19
West Ham United	13 visits	5 wins, 3 draws, 5 defeats	18
Everton	15 visits	4 wins, 3 draws, 8 defeats	15
Sunderland	7 visits	4 wins, 3 draws, 0 defeats	15
Sheffield Wednesday	7 visits	3 wins, 3 draws, 1 defeat	12
Arsenal	15 visits	3 wins, 2 draws, 10 defeats	11
Coventry City	8 visits	3 wins, 2 draws, 3 defeats	11
Blackburn Rovers	13 visits	2 wins, 4 draws, 7 defeats	10
Derby County	7 visits	3 wins, 1 draw, 3 defeats	10
Leicester City	8 visits	2 wins, 4 draws, 2 defeats	10
Bolton Wanderers	9 visits	3 wins, 0 draws, 6 defeats	9
Crystal Palace	3 visits	3 wins, 0 draws, 0 defeats	9
Fulham	7 visits	3 wins, 0 draws, 4 defeats	9
Birmingham City	5 visits	1 win, 4 draws, 0 defeats	7
Charlton Athletic	8 visits	1 win, 4 draws, 3 defeats	7
Ipswich Town	4 visits	2 wins, 1 draw, 1 defeat	7
Manchester City	10 visits	1 win, 4 draws, 5 defeats	7
Nottingham Forest	4 visits	1 win, 3 draws, 0 defeats	6
Queens Park Rangers	3 visits	2 wins, 0 draws, 1 defeat	6
Southampton	12 visits	1 win, 3 draws, 8 defeats	6

Liverpool	15 visits	1 win, 2 draws, 12 defeats	5
Manchester United	15 visits	0 wins, 5 draws, 10 defeats	5
West Bromwich Albion	3 visits	1 win, 2 draws, 0 defeats	5
Chelsea	15 visits	0 wins, 4 draws, 11 defeats	4
Portsmouth	5 visits	0 wins, 4 draws, 1 defeat	4
Wimbledon	7 visits	0 wins, 4 draws, 3 defeats	4
Norwich City	3 visits	1 win, 0 draws, 2 defeats	3
Oldham Athletic	1 visit	1 win, 0 draws, 0 defeats	3
Sheffield United	2 visits	1 win, 0 draws, 1 defeat	3
Watford	2 visits	0 wins, 2 draws, 0 defeats	2
Barnsley	1 visit	0 wins, 1 draw, 0 defeats	1
Bradford City	2 visits	0 wins, 1 draw, 1 defeat	1
Swindon Town	1 visit	0 wins, 1 draw, 0 defeats	1
Wolverhampton Wanderers	1 visit	0 wins, 1 draw, 0 defeats	1
Reading	2 visits	0 wins, 0 draws, 2 defeats	0
Wigan Athletic	3 visits	0 wins, 0 draws, 3 defeats	0
Wigan Athletic	2 visits	0 wins, 0 draws, 2 defeats	0

— BLACK AND WHITE TV —

August 22nd 1964 saw the opening fixtures of the new football season and the debut of a new Saturday evening programme on BBC2, entitled *Match of The Day*. The debut transmission brought the nation highlights of the Division One match at Anfield, where reigning champions Liverpool overcame Arsenal 3–2.

Audience reaction was positive and within months the programme had branched out to cover the occasional lower league fixture. That policy brought fresh-faced young presenter Frank Bough and the cameras to a muddy Brisbane Road on February 20th 1965, to record Leyton Orient's home clash with Second Division leaders Newcastle United. Not for the last time though, Newcastle supporters endured a trial by TV, Joe Elwood netting twice for the Os to cancel out Ron McGarry's penalty.

The BBC then ignored the promoted Magpies in the following season, before covering them once again as they travelled to London in October 1966 – *Match of the Day* having by now graduated to BBC1. Unfortunately, things were little better, Arsenal beating the Toon at Highbury through a Michael Boot effort and a Frank Clark own goal.

A first visit by the cameras to St James' Park came two days before Christmas 1967, Newcastle earning a point in a 1–1 draw with Liverpool. Jimmy Scott scored for the Magpies, Ian St.John netting for the visitors.

Finally, after a televised 0–0 draw at Highbury in February 1968, Newcastle at last tasted victory in front of a nationwide TV audience for the first time on April 12th 1969, as a 'Pop' Robson penalty and Alan Foggon's strike accounted for Manchester United in front of an exuberant Tyneside crowd.

Newcastle's *Match of the Day* debut in colour came in September 1970, when two 'Pop' Robson goals were enough to beat West Ham at Upton Park.

— AWAY FROM THE NUMBERS —

As well as becoming professional footballers, a number of Newcastle United players have shown talent in other branches of sport, including:

Roy Aitken	Basketball
William Aitken	Sprinting
John Anderson	Gaelic Football
John Bailey	Boxing
Jimmy Boyd	Indoor Bowls
Jesse Carver	Weightlifting
David Edgar	Ice Hockey
Tommy Ghee	Water Polo
Chris Guthrie	Fly Fishing
Bobby Moncur	Yachting
Archie Mowatt	Cycling
Ron McGarry	Rugby League
Tommy Pearson	Golf
Jamie Scott	Pole Vaulting
Nigel Walker	Rugby Union
Ron Williams	Crown Green Bowls

— NO CUP OF CHEER —

Milk Cup or Littlewoods, Rumbelows, Coca Cola, Worthington or Carling Cup – call it what you like the 52-year history of the League Cup has been mostly miserable for the Magpies.

Although the competition was first staged in the 1960/61 season, Newcastle actually failed to register a victory until some three years later, a win over Preston North End halting a run of four defeats and two draws.

Of 129 ties played to the start of the 2012/13 season, in the club's complete League Cup history the Magpies have won 58 matches, drawn 18 and lost 53, scoring 207 times and conceding 182 goals (not including penalty shoot-outs).

Newcastle have both scored and conceded seven goals in a League Cup match: enduring a 2–7 reverse at Old Trafford against Manchester United in 1976 and registering a 7–1 success at Meadow Lane against Notts County in 1993.

— SHOOT-OUT FAILURES —

Before beating Watford on penalties in the League Cup 2006, Newcastle had lost all seven of their previous competitive shoot-outs:

Year	Opponent	Competition
1971	Pecsi Dozsa	Inter-Cities Fairs Cup
1979	Sunderland	League Cup
1992	AFC Bournemouth	FA Cup
1996	Chelsea	FA Cup
1998	Blackburn Rovers	League Cup
2002	Everton	League Cup
2003	Partizan Belgrade	Champions League Qualifier

— SHOOT-OUT TRIUMPH —

An instantly forgettable 2006/07 season for Newcastle United was memorable for one achievement – the breaking of a competitive penalty shoot-out hoodoo that had extended over 35 years.

November 7th 2006 saw the Magpies in League Cup fourth round action at Premiership rivals Watford. But after 90 minutes of normal time and an extra half hour left the two sides locked at 2–2, Newcastle faced their eighth competitive penalty shoot-out – having lost the previous seven. With Nolberto Solano stepping up to take the first kick, here's how history was made:

Newcastle:			Watford:		
Solano	scored	1–0	Henderson	scored	5–1

Milner	saved	1–1	Young	missed	1–1
Emre	scored	2–1	Spring	scored	2–2
Duff	scored	3–2	Bangura	scored	3–3
Carr	scored	4–3	Bouazza	scored	4–4
N'Zogbia	scored	5–4	Stewart	saved	5–4

Goalkeeper Steve Harper saved the 12th spot-kick to deny Jordan Stewart, before celebrating with the travelling fans behind him in the Vicarage Road Stand.

— THE WIT AND WISDOM OF SIR BOBBY ROBSON —

"Tickets are selling like cream cakes"

"Rob Lee didn't have a number. Shearer was out of favour. There was no discipline. Players were going upstairs to eat whenever they wanted, using mobile phones whenever they wanted, the whole thing needed an overhaul."
Early days in the Newcastle job

"If we invite any player up to the Quayside to see the girls and then up to our magnificent stadium, we will be able to persuade any player to sign."
The attractions of Tyneside

"We can't replace Gary Speed. Where do you get an experienced player like him with a left foot and a head?"
A quick anatomy lesson

"If you see him stripped, he's like Mike Tyson. But he doesn't bite like Tyson."
Talking about Titus Bramble

"All right, Bellamy came on at Liverpool and did well, but everybody thinks that he's the saviour, he's Jesus Christ. He's not Jesus Christ."
Playing down the cult of Craig

"I handled Bellamy for four years. Graeme Souness couldn't stick four months."
More Craig claims

"We mustn't be despondent. We don't have to play them every week – although we do play them next week as it happens."
Having lost 2–0 to Arsenal, Newcastle prepared to face them in the FA Cup just days later.

"They can't be monks – we don't want them to be monks, we want them to be football players because a monk doesn't play football at this level."
Responding in somewhat bizarre fashion to criticism of player discipline

"When he gets his legs in tandem with his body, we'll make him a player."
On Shola Ameobi

"Tickets are selling like cream cakes."
Before a big match

"We didn't get the rub of the dice."
Mixing his metaphors

"There's a smell of the north-east which drew me back. I've got black

and white blood and I'll stick at it because this is the team I love. I've got a big emotional feeling about it."
Smells like Toon Spirit, Bobby

"We are getting criticised for everything at the moment. There are knives going in my back and arrows flying around my head. But I don't think some people have any idea what we have had to do to keep the ship solvent."
Fighting for the Toon Army . . . the navy and the air force

"As for me, I still love it and I need it. I am more than ready for the challenge and I am determined to win at least one more trophy before I gallop off into the sunset."
Refuting retirement talk

"I say I'm almost over it but it will always rankle. I'll never forget what they did."
In unforgiving mood after his dismissal (1)

"I was kept in the dark with contracts and even transfers. Alex Ferguson, Arsène Wenger and Jose Mourinho know exactly what's going on at their clubs. That doesn't seem possible at Newcastle."
In unforgiving mood after his dismissal (2)

"My dad taught me the value of money and not to throw it away. My players have fame, adoration, money, women, fast cars and no mortgage . . . in the real world, they'd be lucky to get £20,000 a year, never mind a week."
Telling his players a few home truths

— BLACK AND WHITE RIBBONS ON IT —

Despite failing to win the FA Cup since 1955, Newcastle remain inextricably linked with the world's oldest knockout competition.

Although both East End and West End had participated previously, Newcastle United made their FA Cup bow in January 1893, suffering a 2–3 home defeat at the hands of Middlesbrough.

Since that disappointing debut, the club have gone on to lift the trophy on six occasions, been beaten finalists seven more times and endured four unsuccessful appearances in the semi-finals.

However, the former final venue of Crystal Palace wasn't one that agreed with the Magpies, five visits to Sydenham in South London producing three defeats and two draws.

Final successes:

Season	Score	Opponent	Venue
1909/10	1–1	Barnsley	Crystal Palace, London
1909/10 (replay)	2–0	Barnsley	Goodison Park, Liverpool
1923/24	2–0	Aston Villa	Wembley
1931/32	2–1	Arsenal	Wembley
1950/51	2–0	Blackpool	Wembley
1951/52	1–0	Arsenal	Wembley
1954/55	3–1	Manchester City	Wembley

— YOUNGEST/OLDEST —

The appearance of Steve Watson from the substitute's bench during a Second Division game against Wolves in November 1990 saw the defender/midfielder become the youngest player to appear in a competitive senior fixture for Newcastle. North Shields-born Watson was 16 years seven months and nine days old when Manager Jim Smith brought him on to replace Liam O'Brien at Molineux. However, United lost 1–2.

The record had been previously held by Paul Ferris, who was some three months older than Watson when replacing Chris Waddle during a 1–4 loss to Blackburn Rovers at Ewood Park in May 1982.

January 2007 then saw a new record come close to being set, when manager Glenn Roeder named Kazenga LuaLua among his replacements for an FA Cup third-round tie against Birmingham City. That game fell less than a month after the winger had celebrated his 16th birthday, but he remained an unused substitute at St Andrews that day and wouldn't make his first-team bow for another 12 months. Had LuaLua taken the record that day, he would have neatly dovetailed with the oldest player ever to wear a Newcastle shirt in anger – who set the record on the same ground just shy of 80 years earlier. Right-back Billy Hampson was 42 years, seven months and 14 days old when he made his 174th and final senior appearance, during a 0–2 loss at Birmingham April 1927.

Hampson also holds the record for the oldest scorer, and he was 39 years, two months and one day old in October 1923 when he struck from the penalty spot during a 3–2 home victory against Middlesbrough in Division One – his only goal for the club.

Jackie Rutherford remains the youngest scorer, finding the net during a 4–1 top-flight win over Bolton Wanderers at St James' Park in March 1902. The Percy Main-born outside right was aged 17 years, four months and 21 days and making his senior-team debut against the Trotters.

— NEWCASTLE LEGENDS: HUGHIE GALLACHER —

Hughie of the magic feet

Do you ken Hughie Gallacher the wee Scotch Lad?
The best centre forward Newcastle ever had
Contemporary children's rhyme

Having seen him net both goals for Scotland in an international match against England at Hampden Park in May 1925, Newcastle moved to sign Airdrieonians forward Hughie Gallacher.

However, it took the Magpies six months of protracted negotiations and a £6,500 transfer fee to land the diminutive but prolific 22-year-old goalscorer from Lanarkshire.

Gallacher netted twice on his debut in December 1925 as Newcastle drew 3–3 with Everton at St James' Park (Everton taking a point thanks to three goals from striker Dixie Dean, who Newcastle had attempted to sign before turning their attention to Gallacher).

Before leaving Tyneside in 1930, Gallacher gave the public four and a half goal-filled seasons – notching over 20 goals in each campaign he played in.

Captain of the side during the 1926/27 championship-winning season, Gallacher's goals failed to bring further success to the club, and he fell foul of Newcastle's board of directors after a number of on-field clashes with both referees and opponents.

There was also the little matter of a colourful off-field lifestyle that saw him mix with supporters in local bars, dance halls and on occasion, Magistrates Courts.

After keeping a declining Newcastle side in the First Division, Gallacher was sold to Chelsea in May 1930 for £10,000 amid an outcry from supporters. A record attendance of almost 69,000 packed St James' to see Gallacher return with the Londoners in September of that year, although United's Jackie Cape deviated from the script by scoring the only goal of the game.

Gallacher was to return to Tyneside in 1938 after having appeared for Derby County, Notts County and Grimsby Town. He played one final season for Gateshead before settling in the town and holding down a variety of jobs, including a stint as a football writer.

And it was in Gateshead that he chose to take his own life, walking out in front of an approaching train in June 1957, having been called to appear in court to answer charges of maltreating his son.

Hughie Gallacher factfile
Born: Bellshill, north Lanarkshire, February 2nd 1903
Died: June 11th 1957
Newcastle career: 174 apps, 143 goals (1925–30)
Other clubs: Queen of the South, Airdrie, Chelsea, Derby County, Notts County, Grimsby Town, Gateshead
International: Scotland, 19 caps, 22 goals

— HOT SHOTS —

Newcastle United's top scorers in all competitive games:

Rank	Player	League	Cup	Total
1.	Alan Shearer	148	58	206
2.	Jackie Milburn	177	23	200
3.	Len White	142	11	153
4.	Hughie Gallacher	133	10	143

5.	Malcolm Macdonald	95	26	121
6.	Peter Beardsley	108	11	119
7.=	Bobby Mitchell	95	18	113
7.=	Tom McDonald	100	13	113
9.	Neil Harris	87	14	101
10.	Bryan 'Pop' Robson	82	15	97

— HUMAN BILLBOARDS —

The Magpies wore shirt advertising for the first time in 1980, with the Newcastle Breweries Blue Star logo appearing on the front of home and away shirts.

However, if match highlights were televised advertising was banned, so the presence of TV cameras at the opening day trip to Hillsborough saw Newcastle wearing unadorned yellow shirts.

The Blue Star debuted in a home draw with Notts County in August 1980, having also been worn at Gallowgate in a friendly against Leeds United earlier that month.

With shirt advertising still frowned upon by the FA, Newcastle were fined £1,000 for wearing strips with the logo in January 1981 against Sheffield Wednesday – even though the FA Cup tie wasn't televised.

Subsequent seasons saw the Blue Star continue to be used, until the brewer's deal expired at the end of the 1985/86 season.

Their replacements were Warrington-based brewer Greenall Whitley, who were looking to extend into the north-east. Shirts appeared emblazoned with 'Greenall's Beers' and a lifting of the TV ban extended the coverage.

The following seasons saw the word 'Beers' dropped from the shirts, before the deal ended after a home draw with Swindon Town in December 1990.

Three days later came the return of Newcastle Breweries and a Blue Star logo on the home kits and black 'McEwan's Lager' lettering on the away shirt. Fans owning now-obsolete Greenalls replica shirts were offered free Blue Star patches to mask the old advertisers!

The next change came in the opening weeks of the 1993/94 season, when home shirts appeared with 'McEwan's Lager' lettering in gold. These gave way to a white on black version of the same design, alternating with the Blue Star – an arrangement continuing into the following season. 1995, though, saw the Blue Star design downsized and relegated to use only on the away kit.

The Newcastle Brown Ale bottle logo replaced it on the home shirts, proving an instant hit and selling in unprecedented quantities. This had an early pre-season airing at Hartlepool in July 1995. That classic logo then survived numerous shirt design changes before a farewell in May 2000 as the brewery sponsorship ended with a home win against Arsenal.

There was one oddity in this era, however. An on-air alcohol advertising ban on French TV led Newcastle to wear shirts advertising holiday park brand 'Centerparcs' for their European tie at Monaco (logo-free shirts had been worn earlier that season in Metz).

Season 2000/01 saw cable TV company NTL's logo then appear on shirts, as part of a deal by which they acquired a stake in the club. When that ended after three seasons, however, the club inked a new deal with Tyneside-based building society, Northern Rock.

The banking crisis of 2007 then saw Northern Rock taken into state ownership – a move which had no effect on the agreement to sponsor the club, but which caused some jibes among media commentators and rival supporters. The announcement of an extended sponsorship deal in 2010 then further raised eyebrows, given that the club was in effect sponsored by HM Government.

January 2012 then saw the Magpies take to the field against Manchester United at St James' Park wearing black and white shirts with hastily-applied "Virgin Money" logos obscuring the previous Northern Rock branding. That followed the completion of a deal by Virgin to purchase Northern Rock from the government, followed by a two-year shirt sponsorship arrangement.

A week later Sir Richard Branson then donned a shirt on a visit to Tyneside, but exposed his lack of football knowledge by telling reporters that, "We did the sponsorship deal two hours before the match, got the name on the shirts and they beat Manchester United three-love."

As had been the case back in 1991, replacement patches were distributed by the club for those supporters who wished to similarly update their replica shirts in mid-season.

— TRANSFER TRAIL II —

In chronological order, the record transfer fees received for Newcastle players are:

Player	Year	Fee	Received from
Bobby Templeton	1904	£375	Woolwich Arsenal
Albert Shepherd	1914	£1,500	Bradford City
Hughie Gallacher	1930	£10,000	Chelsea
Albert Stubbins	1946	£12,500	Liverpool
Len Shackleton	1948	£20,050	Sunderland
Ernie Taylor	1951	£25,000	Blackpool
George Eastham	1960	£47,500	Arsenal
Alan Suddick	1966	£63,000	Blackpool
Bryan Robson	1971	£120,000	West Ham United
Terry McDermott	1974	£170,000	Liverpool
Malcolm Macdonald	1976	£333,333	Arsenal
Irving Nattrass	1979	£375,000	Middlesbrough
Peter Withe	1980	£500,000	Aston Villa
Chris Waddle	1985	£590,000	Tottenham Hotspur
Peter Beardsley	1987	£1,900,000	Liverpool
Paul Gascoigne	1988	£2,300,000	Tottenham Hotspur
Andy Cole	1995	£7,000,000	Manchester United
Dietmar Hamann	1999	£7,500,000	Liverpool
Jonathan Woodgate	2004	£13,667,000	Real Madrid
Andy Carroll	2011	£35,000,000	Liverpool

— EARLY DOORS —

On Saturday January 18th 2003, Kevin Keegan's Manchester City side visited St James' Park with former Newcastle defenders Steve Howey and Sylvain Distin lining up for the visitors. Just before kick-off Alan Shearer was presented with the Goal of the Month award for a rapier strike against Everton the previous month – and was soon to be hogging the limelight again.

The match got underway with City defending the Leazes End and after kicking off, Howey played the ball back towards his goalkeeper Carlo Nash. Enter Shearer, who raced in and charged down Nash's attempted clearance before passing the ball into the unguarded net. The goal was timed at 10.4 seconds, with no other Newcastle player having touched the ball.

Newcastle went on to win the game 2–0, but Shearer's goal dominated the post-match coverage, being confirmed as the quickest strike of his career and the club's fastest-ever goal in top-flight football.

However, Jackie Milburn's effort in a Second Division game against Cardiff City on November 22nd 1947 is unofficially believed to be the fastest competitive goal for the club. No confirmed measure of the goal time exists, but the goalscorer himself later gave it as six seconds. The Magpies went on to win that match 4–1.

It was quickly established via TV replays that Shearer had just missed out on the record for the fastest ever Premiership goal. That accolade is held by Tottenham defender Ledley King, who netted in a fraction less than 10 seconds in a 3–3 draw against Bradford City at Valley Parade on December 9th 2000.

"I didn't think I had the legs to run half the length of the pitch in 10 seconds. I certainly couldn't have done it late in the game," said Shearer after the game.

— SUPERMAC'S QUICKFIRE GOAL —

Anecdotal evidence gives Malcolm Macdonald the record of scoring the fastest-ever goal in a public match involving the Newcastle first team. That happened at the start of a 7–3 pre-season friendly win over Scottish side St Johnstone on July 29th 1972.

Spotting Saints goalkeeper Derek Robertson still going through his warm-up routine, Macdonald took John Tudor's pass from the kick-off and netted from just inside the St Johnstone half – the goal unofficially timed at four seconds.

— CORNERS OF A FOREIGN FIELD —

Since Newcastle made their away bow in Rotterdam on a Tuesday night back in September 1969, up until the start of the 2008/09 season the club have played 60 away ties in various European competitions. In those games, the Magpies have played in 24 countries against 53 sides in 52 different stadia:

Season/competition	Opponent	Venue
1968/69 Fairs Cup	Feyenoord	De Kuip Stadion, Rotterdam

1968/69 Fairs Cup	Sporting Lisbon	Arvelade Stadium, Lisbon
1968/69 Fairs Cup	Real Zaragoza	Romareda Stadium, Zaragoza
1968/69 Fairs Cup	Vitoria Setubal	Arvelade Stadium, Lisbon
1968/69 Fairs Cup	Glasgow Rangers	Ibrox Park, Glasgow
1968/69 Fairs Cup	Ujpesti Dozsa	Megyeri uti Stadion, Budapest
1969/70 Fairs Cup	Dundee United	Tannadice Park, Dundee
1969/70 Fairs Cup	FC Porto	Estadio das Antas, Porto
1969/70 Fairs Cup	Southampton	The Dell, Southampton
1969/70 Fairs Cup	Anderlecht	Parc Astrid, Brussels
1970/71 Fairs Cup	Inter Milan	Giuseppe Meazza, Milan
1970/71 Fairs Cup	Pecsi Dozsa	Pecsi Vasutas Sport Kor, Pecs
1977/78 UEFA Cup	Bohemians	Dalymount Park, Dublin
1977/78 UEFA Cup	SEC Bastia	Stade Armand Cesari de Furiani
1994/95 UEFA Cup	Royal Antwerp	Bosuil Stadion, Antwerp
1994/95 UEFA Cup	Atletico Bilbao	San Mames, Bilbao
1996/97 UEFA Cup	Halmstads	Orjans vall Stadion, Halmstad
1996/97 UEFA Cup	Ferencvaros	Ulloi uti Stadion, Budapest
1996/97 UEFA Cup	AS Metz	Stade Saint-Symphorien, Metz
1996/97 UEFA Cup	AS Monaco	Stade Louis II, Monaco
1997/98 Champions League	Croatia Zagreb	Maksimir Stadium, Zagreb
1997/98 Champions League	Dynamo Kiev	Olympic Stadium, Kiev
1997/98 Champions League	PSV Eindhoven	Philips Stadium, Eindhoven
1997/98 Champions League	Barcelona	Nou Camp, Barcelona
1998/89 Cup Winner's Cup	Partizan Belgrade	JNA Stadium, Belgrade
1999/00 UEFA Cup	CSKA Sofia	Balgarska Armia, Sofia
1999/00 UEFA Cup	Zurich	Letzigrund, Zurich
1999/00 UEFA Cup	AS Roma	Olympic Stadium, Rome
2001/02 Intertoto Cup	Sporting Lokeren	Daknam Stadium, Lokeren
2001/02 Intertoto Cup	1860 Munich	Olympic Stadium, Munich

2001/02 Intertoto Cup	Troyes	Stade de l'Aube, Troyes
2002/03 Champions League	NK Zeljeznicar	Kosevo Stadium, Sarajevo
2002/03 Champions League	Dynamo Kiev	Olympic Stadium, Kiev
2002/03 Champions League	Juventus	Stadio Delle Alpi, Turin
2002/03 Champions League	Feyenoord	De Kuip Stadion, Rotterdam
2002/03 Champions League	Barcelona	Nou Camp, Barcelona
2002/03 Champions League	Bayer Leverkusen	BayArena, Leverkusen
2002/03 Champions League	Inter Milan	Giuseppe Meazza, Milan
2003/04 Champions League	Partizan Belgrade	JNA Stadium, Belgrade
2003/04 UEFA Cup	NAC Breda	MyCom Stadium, Breda
2003/04 UEFA Cup	FC Basel	St Jakob Park, Basel
2003/04 UEFA Cup	Valerenga IF	Ullevaal Stadium, Oslo
2003/04 UEFA Cup	Real Mallorca	Estadi Son Moix, Palma
2003/04 UEFA Cup	PSV Eindhoven	Phillips Stadium, Eindhoven
2003/04 UEFA Cup	Olympique de Marseille	Stade Velodrome, Marseille
2004/05 UEFA Cup	Hapoel Bnei Sakhnin	Ramat Gan Stadium, Tel Aviv
2004/05 UEFA Cup	Panionios	Nea Smyrni Stadium, Athens
2004/05 UEFA Cup	Sochaux	Stade Auguste Bonal, Sochaux
2004/05 UEFA Cup	Heerenveen	Abe Lenstra Stadium, H'veen
2004/05 UEFA Cup	Olympiakos	Karaiskakis Stadium, Athens
2004/05 UEFA Cup	Sporting Lisbon	Arvelade Stadium, Lisbon
2005/06 Intertoto Cup	FK ZTS Dubnica	Mestsky Stadium, Dubnica
2005/06 Intertoto Cup	Deportivo La Coruna	Riazor Stadium, La Coruna

2006/07	Intertoto Cup	Lillestrom	Arasen Stadium, Oslo
2006/07	UEFA Cup	FK Ventspils	Skonto Stadium, Riga
2006/07	UEFA Cup	Levadia Tallinn	A. Le Coq Arena, Tallinn
2006/07	UEFA Cup	Palermo	Renzo Barbera, Palermo
2006/07	UEFA Cup	Eintracht Frankfurt	Commerzbank Arena, Frankfurt
2006/07	UEFA Cup	Zulte Waregem	Jules Otten Stadium, Ghent
2006/07	UEFA Cup	AZ Alkmaar	DSB Stadium, Alkmaar

— SEMI SUCCESS —

The full list of the club's semi-final triumphs:

Season	Score	Opponent	Venue
1904/05	1–0	Sheffield Wednesday	Hyde Road, Manchester
1905/06	2–0	Arsenal	Victoria Ground, Stoke
1907/08	6–0	Fulham	Anfield, Liverpool
1909/10	2–0	Swindon Town	White Hart Lane, London
1910/11	3–0	Chelsea	St.Andrews', Birmingham
1923/24	2–0	Manchester City	St.Andrews'
1931/32	2–1	Chelsea	Leeds Road, Huddersfield
1950/51	0–0	Wolverhampton Wanderers	Hillsborough, Sheffield
1950/51 (replay)	2–0	Wolverhampton Wanderers	Leeds Road
1951/52	0–0	Blackburn Rovers	Hillsborough
1951/52 (replay)	2–0	Blackburn Rovers	Elland Road, Leeds
1954/55	1–1	York City	Hillsborough
1954/55 (replay)	2–0	York City	Roker Park, Sunderland
1973/74	2–0	Burnley	Hillsborough
1997/98	1–0	Sheffield United	Old Trafford, Manchester
1998/99	2–0	Tottenham Hotspur	Old Trafford, Manchester

— DOUBLE AGENTS —

"This for me is the derby to end all derbies. It can rival Glasgow and is more passionate than Manchester, Liverpool and certainly London.

Other derbies have never generated such huge feeling, such elation and deep gloom."
Bobby Moncur (who played on both sides) summing up the mood that envelops the region when Newcastle United and Sunderland face each on the field.

As well as Moncur, other players to have appeared in senior football for both sides are:

William Agnew	Stan Anderson
John Auld	Harry Bedford
Paul Bracewell	Titus Bramble
Michael Bridges	Ivor Broadis
Alan Brown	Steve Caldwell
Johnny Campbell	Michael Chopra
Jeff Clarke	Lee Clark
Andy Cole	Joe Devine
John Dowsey	Robbie Elliott
Dave Elliott	Ray Ellison
Alan Foggon	Howard Gayle
Tommy Gibb	Shay Given
Thomas Grey	Ron Guthrie
Tom Hall	Mick Harford
Steve Hardwick	John Harvey
David Kelly	Alan Kennedy
James Logan	Andy McCombie
Bob McDermid	Albert McInroy
Bob McKay	Bobby Moncur
James Raine	Bobby Robinson
Ray Robinson	Bryan Robson
Tom Rowlandson	Len Shackleton
Jock Smith	Colin Suggett
Ernie Taylor	Bob Thomson
Thomas Urwin	Barry Venison
Chris Waddle	Nigel Walker
Billy Whitehurst	Dave Willis
David Young	

In addition, the following players guested in War Leagues during WW2:

Walter Boyes
Norman Coyde
Len Duns

Patsy Gallacher
Alex Lockie
Cec McCormack
Jackie Milburn
Stan Mortensen
Bill Nicholson
Jackie Robinson
Fred Smallwood
Johnny Spuhler
Albert Stubbins
Ken Walshaw

—THE LEAZES —

Named after the Castle Leazes site that St James' Park was built on, generations of Newcastle supporters cheered on the lads under the shelter of the covered terrace erected in 1929 – the only part of renowned stadium architect Archibald Leitch's grand design for St James' Park to be constructed.

Replacing the first banked standing accommodation at that north end of the ground constructed 30 years earlier, the new roofed enclosure accommodated 15,000 and was constructed by Bewley & Scott of Gateshead.

The Leazes housed most of the club's hardcore support, who provided vocal encouragement to their heroes and intimidation of opponents. This was the home of the Geordie roar, the so-called "Twelfth Man".

Closing after a midweek 2–2 draw with Manchester City in March 1978, the bulldozers immediately moved in to demolish the structure as part of a plan to extend the East Stand around to the north end of the stadium. However, funding issues following the club's relegation meant that redevelopment went no further than construction of some retaining walls, turnstiles and uncovered terraces far smaller than what had been swept away.

Shared by home and away supporters and on occasions given over entirely to visiting fans, the Leazes was fenced in (along with the Gallowgate End and West Stand) between 1983 and 1988. Temporary uncovered seating (borrowed from a motor racing circuit) was erected over part of the Leazes End during the 1987/88 campaign, accommodating season ticket holders displaced from the West Stand by the construction of the new Milburn Stand.

Stadium legislation and belated investment in the club brought about the long-awaited Leazes redevelopment in 1993, with a new stand containing over 11,000 seats debuting when United made a losing start to life in the Premier League against Spurs in August 1993. November 1993 then saw club Chairman Sir John Hall name the Leazes End Stand after himself, burying a time capsule including a bottle of Newcastle Brown Ale. And by May 1994, the Leazes Stand was complete and connected to both the East and Milburn Stands.

That first rebuild, though, survived only until 1999, when plans to increase the capacity of the stadium from 36,000 to 52,000 saw the removal of the Leazes roof and the addition of another tier, extending along the entire length of the Milburn Stand (later christened Level Seven).

The newly completed stadium was then inaugurated with a 3–2 victory over Derby County in August 2000, with a total capacity of 52,243.

— MCC: MAGPIES CRICKET CLUB —

It's appropriate that a club which can trace their origins back to local cricket sides (see *From Eastenders to West End Boys*, page 1) should have signed a number of players who also showed some prowess with bat and ball.

Here's a Newcastle United XI made up of players who also shone in all white:

Player	On the books of
James Beaumont	Leicestershire
Kevin Brock	Wark (Northumberland League)
Ian Davies	Somerset
Harry Hardinge	Kent
Steve Harper	Easington (Durham Leagues)
Keith Kettleborough	Rotherham Town (Yorkshire League)
John Mitten	Leicestershire, Nottinghamshire, Lancashire
Peter Ramage	Tynemouth (North-East League)
Malcolm Scott	Northamptonshire
Arthur Turner	Hampshire
Sam Weaver	Derbyshire, Somerset

A willing 12th man for this imaginary side would be England pace bowler Steve Harmison, who cured his injury woes under the expert eyes of the Newcastle United medical staff. Magpies season ticket holder

Harmison has gone on record as saying he'd willingly have given up cricket had he been given the opportunity to play professional football.

And the man nicknamed 'Toon Harmy' has appeared for the Magpies, lining up in 2005 alongside the likes of Robbie Elliott and Peter Ramage in a training ground friendly against the celebrity XI preparing for the Sky TV *The Match* series.

Barring an unexpected playing contract for Harmison though, the only player to have represented Newcastle United and played test match cricket remains Harry Hardinge – who did so some 13 years after leaving St James' Park.

The batsman widely known as 'Wally' in cricketing circles was selected for England in the Third Test against Australia in July 1921 at Headingley. Hardinge managed a knock of 25 in the first innings but fell after making just five in the second innings. The visiting side won by 219 runs, taking an unassailable 3–0 lead in the five-match series and thus retaining the Ashes.

— ON THE ROAD AGAIN —

By the end of the 2011/12 season, Newcastle had completed a half century of appearances at different stadia in the Premier League, playing 43 different sides in the process. Of these 41, they have played eight teams at two different grounds. They are:

Opponent	Stadia
Arsenal	Highbury, Emirates Stadium
Bolton Wanders	Burnden Park, Reebok Stadium
Derby County	Baseball Ground, Pride Park
Fulham	Craven Cottage, Loftus Road
Leicester City	Filbert Street, Walkers Stadium
Manchester City	Maine Road, City of Manchester Stadium
Southampton	The Dell, St. Mary's Stadium
Sunderland	Roker Park, The Stadium of Light

— NICKNAMES PART I —

A selection of nicknames from the earlier years of Newcastle United's history:

'Daddler'	Andy Aitken
'Cockles	Bill Appleyard

'Knocker'	Thomas Bartlett
'Ankles'	Albert Bennett
'Rock of Tyneside'	Frank Brennan
'Big Sandy'	Alex Caie
'Hughie'	Joe Ford
'Punky'	Alex Gardner
'The Duke'	Doug Graham
'Wally'	Harry Hardinge
'Diddler'	Albert Harris
'Tiger'	Jimmy Hill
'Hurricane Hutch'	Duncan Hutchison
'Camel'	Vic Keeble
'The Laughing Cavalier'	Wilf Low
'Bobby Dazzler'	Bobby Mitchell
'Tucker'	Tom Mordue
'Scots Wullie'	Bill McPhillips
'Peter the Great'	Peter McWilliam
'Clown Prince of Soccer'	Len Shackleton
'Tadger'	Jimmy Stewart
'The Silent Assassin'	Albert Stubbins
'Topper'	Tommy Thompson
'Ginger'	Jack Wilkinson
'Monte'	Johnny Wilkinson

— IT'S WOR CUP . . . SOMETIMES —

Of 365 FA Cup ties played by Newcastle up to the start of the 2012/13 season, United have won 178, drawn 85 and lost 102.

The club's biggest FA Cup victory remains a 9–0 success against Southport in season 1931/32 – this coming after two 1–1 draws in the first two matches of the tie, resulting in this second replay being staged at the neutral venue of Hillsborough, Sheffield.

A 1–7 reverse at Villa Park against Aston Villa in season 1896/97 is Newcastle's heaviest defeat in the competition. Villa went on to complete a League and FA Cup Double.

To date, the Magpies have netted 655 times and conceded 444 goals in the FA Cup (not including penalty shoot-outs).

— NEWCASTLE LEGENDS: TONY GREEN —

TOON LEGENDS

TONY GREEN

Tony Green: Still revered on Tyneside

"It was the saddest day of my life: he was my very best buy. I could watch him play all day and every day." The words of then Newcastle boss Joe Harvey provide some insight into why Tony Green was worshipped by the St James' Park faithful during his brief spell with Newcastle before injury forced his retirement at the age of just 26.

A fantastic combination of speed on the ball, close control and balance had made Green the idol of Bloomfield Road after he joined Blackpool from Albion Rovers in his native Glasgow. Alerted to his promise and goalscoring prowess alongside former Magpie Alan Suddick in the Blackpool midfield, Don Revie tried to sign Green for

Leeds United after he had proved his fitness again following a year-long lay-off through injury.

However, Revie found himself out of the loop when the old boy network smoothed the passage of Green's transfer to St James' – Harvey and Blackpool boss Bob Stokoe were former Newcastle team-mates in the 1950s.

For Harvey, Green's arrival on Tyneside in October 1971 relieved the pressure on a side who had slipped to second from bottom in the league. Green took some of the midfield burden from Terry Hibbitt, helping to provide an improvement in the service to striker Malcolm Macdonald and a subsequent climb up the table.

Blackpool, meanwhile, received £90,000 in cash plus striker Keith Dyson, who Stokoe hoped would boost his side's efforts at achieving promotion from Division Two.

Green became an instant terrace hero in his first season at Newcastle and he collected numerous man of the match awards despite the club's unexceptional eleventh place finish and infamous FA Cup exit at Hereford United.

Of his 27 league appearances that season, the victory at Old Trafford one week after the nightmare on Edgar Street remains one of his most celebrated displays. Although Green didn't score that day, his domination of the midfield was lauded in the press and hopes were high that the following season would see the club challenge for major honours once more.

In the event Harvey's side improved their Division One finishing position by three spots, finishing eighth. However, that was to be achieved largely without the contribution of Green. On September 2nd 1972 he was stretchered off the field at Selhurst Park with a knee injury after a tackle by Crystal Palace hardman Mel Blyth.

Green endured three operations before an abortive comeback in a reserve game at Coventry in November 1973 confirmed the inevitable.

Middlesbrough provided the opposition for a testimonial in May 1974 – almost 30,000 supporters turning out despite having seen Newcastle beaten at Wembley less than a week earlier.

Moving back to the Lancashire coast, Green became a school teacher and served on the Pools Panel. His occasional visits to St James' Park still result in a rousing reception from supporters who remember his brief, but wonderful time in Toon.

Tony Green factfile
Born: Glasgow, October 13th 1946
Newcastle career: 38 apps, 3 goals (1971–73)
Other clubs: Albion Rovers, Blackpool
International: Scotland, 6 caps, 0 goals

— THE GALLOWGATE —

Providing a vantage point from the earliest days of Newcastle United's existence, an earth bank at the south end of St James' Park was constructed in the early 1890s and fitted with barriers made of post and rope in 1905.

Little changed over the following decades, save for the addition of more permanent crash barriers and railings, and the Gallowgate Terrace became the focal point of the club's most vocal fans following the closure of the Leazes End in March 1978.

Divided into three sections, older malcontents were to be found clustered underneath the floodlight pylon at the western end, while another pylon at the opposite eastern end was also overlooked by a large "ten-minute" flag – originally a Union Flag, replaced in later years by a bespoke black-and-white-striped effort which would be refurled when 80 minutes had been played. This came to be known as the Strawberry Corner due to its proximity to the pub of that name, but in general usage it was referred to as simply The Corner.

The centre section, meanwhile, was christened The Scoreboard, following the replacement of an earlier manual display of half-time scores with an electric board in 1980. Never roofed – despite periodic promises from the club – the fans remained open to the elements.

Surviving into the Premier League era, the last hurrah for the Gallowgate Terrace was United's promotion season of 1992/93; the team providing their own memorable sign-off by whacking six first-half goals into the net at that end in the 7–1 season-closer against Leicester City.

Ground redevelopment reached that end of the stadium in early 1994, with the construction of a new stand at that end beginning in early 1994, with a structure mirroring that at the Leazes End rising behind reduced sized standing paddocks. However, the presence of old mine workings and the tunnelling for the metro station added to the complexity of the building project and required the sinking of huge supporting piles – an obstacle that was claimed to preclude any future plans for extending the Level Seven tier round from the Milburn Stand.

The all-seater Gallowgate stand was open for the start of the 1994/95 season – although it took another year for the corner sections to be constructed and form a continuous seating bowl around the pitch for the very first time.

A commercial link-up with the owners of the adjacent Tyne Brewery then saw the newly covered area re-christened the Exhibition Stand (later The Newcastle Brown Ale South Stand). More recently it's reverted to the Gallowgate.

— NEWCASTLE'S TOP 10 FA CUP SCORERS —

Player	Total
Jackie Milburn	23
Alan Shearer	21
Bobby Mitchell	18
Bill Appleyard	16
Albert Shepherd	16
Neil Harris	14
James Howie	14
Malcolm Macdonald	14
John Rutherford	14
Tom McDonald	13

— FRENCH FOREIGN LEGION —

Aside from Englishmen, Newcastle have relied on more French-born players during their 18 Premiership seasons than from any other nation – no fewer than 20 in all:

Player		Signed	From
David Ginola	July 1995	Paris St Germain
Stephane Guivarc'h	June 1998	Auxerre
Laurent Charvet	July 1998	Cannes
Didier Domi	November 1998	Paris St Germain
Louis Saha	January 1999	Metz (loan)
Alain Goma	June 1999	Paris St Germain
Franck Dumas	July 1999	Monaco
Olivier Bernard	September 2000	Olympique Lyonnais

Laurent Robert	August 2001	Paris St.Germain
Sylvain Distin	September 2001	Paris St.Germain (loan)
Charles N'Zogbia	July 2004	Le Havre
Antoine Sibierski	August 2006	Manchester City
Habib Beye	August 2007	Olympique Marseille
Sebastien Bassong	July 2008	Metz
Fabrice Pancrate	November 2009	Unattached
Hatem Ben Arfa	August 2010	Olympique Marseille
Yohan Cabaye	June 2011	Lille OSC
Demba Ba	June 2011	Unattached
Sylvain Marveaux	June 2011	Stade Rennes
Gabriel Obertan	August 2011	Manchester United

The Magpies also signed five further French-born players who failed to make a competitive first-team appearance for the club:

David Terrier	January 1998	Unattached
Lionel Perez	June 1998	Sunderland
Olivier Bernard	September 2006	Unattached
Wesley Ngo Baheng	August 2007	Le Havre
Yven Moyo	September 2010	Sochaux

And one yet to appear in the Premier League but with outings in the FA Cup and Carling Cup:

Mehdi Abeid	July 2011

Bernard was a free agent when he joined Newcastle for a second time in September 2006, his signing outside the transfer window being permissible after he was released from his playing contract with Glasgow Rangers.

— ENGLAND'S DREAMING —

Thirty-five players have appeared in the full England side while being on Newcastle United's books:

Player	Date	Opponent
Matt Kingsley	March 18th 1901	Wales (h)
Jackie Rutherford	April 9th 1904	Scotland (a)
Jack Carr	February 25th 1905	Ireland (h)
Albert Gosnell	February 17th 1906	Ireland (a)
Colin Veitch	February 17th 1906	Ireland (a)

Albert Shepherd	February 11th 1911	Ireland (h)
Jimmy Stewart	April 1st 1911	Scotland (h)
Charlie Spencer	April 12th 1924	Scotland (h)
Frank Hudspeth	October 24th 1925	Northern Ireland (a)
Tom Urwin	March 1st 1926	Wales (h)
Jack Hill	May 9th 1929	France (a)
Samuel Weaver	April 9th 1932	Scotland (h)
Jimmy Richardson	May 13th 1933	Italy (a)
Dave Fairhurst	December 6th 1933	France (h)
Duggie Wright	November 9th 1938	Norway (h)
Jackie Milburn	October 9th 1948	Northern Ireland (a)
Ivor Broadis	April 3rd 1954	Scotland (a)
Malcolm Macdonald	May 20th 1972	Wales (a)
Chris Waddle	March 26th 1985	Republic of Ireland (h)
Peter Beardsley	January 29th 1986	Egypt (a)
Rob Lee	October 12th 1994	Romania (h)
Steve Howey	November 16th 1994	Nigeria (h)
Barry Venison	September 7th 1994	USA (h)
Warren Barton	June 8th 1995	Sweden (h)
Les Ferdinand	December 12th 1995	Portugal (h)
Alan Shearer	September 1st 1996	Moldova (a)
David Batty	September 1st 1996	Moldova (a)
Kieron Dyer	September 4th 1999	Luxembourg (h)
Jermaine Jenas	February 12th 2003	Australia (h)
Jonathan Woodgate	March 31st 2004	Sweden (a)
Nicky Butt	August 18th 2004	Ukraine (h)
Michael Owen	September 7th 2005	Northern Ireland (a)
Scott Parker	October 11th 2006	Croatia (a)
Alan Smith	August 22nd 2007	Germany (h)
Andy Carroll	November 17th 2010	France (h)

Note: the dates and opponents given are the first appearance as a Magpie and therefore not necessarily the player's actual England debut.

Of these players, six marked that first appearance by scoring: Albert Shepherd, Jimmy Stewart, Jackie Milburn, Ivor Broadis, Rob Lee and Alan Shearer.

Meanwhile, Matt Kingsley, Duggie Wright and Nicky Butt all enjoyed the comfort of their England debut as a Newcastle player being staged at St James' Park.

Not included in the list is Paul Gascoigne, who made his England debut while a Tottenham Hotspur player in September 1988 – having moved from Newcastle just two months previously.

— BUY OR SELL ANY SPARES —

The first all-ticket FA Cup final was the 1924 meeting between Newcastle United and Aston Villa – the decision being taken following the chaos of the 'White Horse Final' between Bolton and West Ham 12 months previously when thousands of fans spilled onto the pitch delaying the start.

— MEMORY MATCHES 5 —

February 5th 2011

Newcastle 4 Arsenal 4 (Premier League)

Having scored four goals without reply in a Carling Cup tie at St James' Park earlier in the season, the Gunners were quickly into their stride in the league meeting Theo Walcott raced away for the opener after just 41 seconds. Johan Djourou made it 0–2 less than two minutes later, Robin van Persie made it 0–3 on ten minutes and then headed a fourth after just 26 minutes, as the Arsenal fans sang, "You might as well go home."

Shell-shocked from what they had seen – ending a week in which Andy Carroll had controversially been sold to Liverpool and United meekly surrendered at Fulham – a few home supporters took their advice. However, most stayed on and witnessed one of the most incredible turnarounds ever seen at Gallowgate. The trigger was a 50th-minute clash between Joey Barton and Abou Diaby, with referee Phil Dowd showing yellow then red as the Frenchman raised his hands to Barton and then team-mate Kevin Nolan in quick succession.

It was hardly enough to convince anyone that a fight back might be on the cards but when Leon Best was fouled by Laurent Koscielny in the box on 68 minutes, Barton stroked the spot kick past Wojciech

Szcz sny. Leon Best then saw a valid-looking effort ruled out before poking home Jose Enrique's centre. It was 2–4 with 15 m inutes remaining and the crowd were in full voice – sensing nervousness among Arsene Wenger's ten men.

Linesman Trevor Massey then called a foul on United defender Mike Williamson in the box and a second, less convincing spot kick conversion from Barton made it 3–4 on 83 minutes. With former favourite Tino Asprilla watching on, Newcastle then summoned up an equaliser with a strike of simply stunning quality, Cheick Tiote scoring his first goal for the club with a fabulous volley that screamed into the corner of the Gallowgate End net with three minutes to play.

Even more improbably, Nolan and then shot across goal with the 'keeper beaten, before a manic five minutes of added time saw both teams come close to grabbing a winner. Manager Alan Pardew later admitted that his half time team talk included the comment; "You can't sulk in front of 52,000 at St James' Park."

NUFC: Harper, Simpson, Enrique, Williamson, Coloccini, Barton, Tiote, Nolan, Best (Guthrie), Lovenkrands (Ranger), Gutierrez.

— POPULAR SIDE —

Still known to many as the "New" Stand – although it's now the oldest visible section of St James' Park – the cantilever construction on the east side of the stadium was designed by Tyneside architects Faulkner Brown and began to take shape in late 1971. However, it took some 16 months to build, partly due to what were termed as "labour difficulties" (strikes in the building trade and fuel shortages) and was almost six months behind schedule when all 3,400 seats were available for the first time in April 1973, for a 2–1 defeat by West Ham.

It replaced an uncovered terrace that in its latter years had a 10,000 capacity and was Popular Side, linking the Gallowgate and Leazes End and allowing the residents of Leazes Terrace behind views of the pitch.

The listed building status of that street meant that design limitations were placed on the club by City Council Planners – similar considerations preventing subsequent enlargement of the facilities on this side of the stadium.

Originally constructed with standing paddocks at pitch side, these were converted to bench seating in the wake of the infamous 1980 petrol bomb attack on West Ham fans, thrown from that section. That alteration, however, did mean that this side of the ground survived the dreaded fences of that decade – unlike the other three sides of the ground.

The first executive boxes in SJP were also constructed at the back of those paddocks, while the first dedicated family section was created. The benches were later converted to individual seats in eye-catching contrasting sections of black and white during the 1990s.

Newcastle United lettering along the upper section of the stand had appeared by the time United took their place in the Premier League, while the later removal of the Executive boxes allowed the club to remodel the East Stand seating deck to be on a level with the new corner stands by the time the newly extended 52,000+ stadium opened for business in 2000.

— BOARD GAMES —

Installed at a cost of £66,000 and paid for by Scottish and Newcastle Breweries, St James' Park's first electronic scoreboard made its debut on December 20th 1980 – hardly being tested by a dull 0–0 draw with Bristol City.

The new stadium feature replaced the previous manually operated cricket-type scoreboard, which displayed half-time scores at other grounds alongside a letter corresponding to listings in the match programme.

However, the new technology allowed for all sorts of 'extras', ranging from a fan-friendly time countdown and announcement of the attendance to rather less practical displays of 'winking eyes' and what looked like an assortment of badly-formed dancing Mister Men.

Sited behind the centre section of the uncovered Gallowgate End, an early design defect was noted by those fans who from time to time chose to climb onto it. The game score display relied on the name of the opponents being added for each game in temporary letters. Unfortunately these proved to be less than robust – leading to unfamiliar opponents such as 'elsea' appearing at St James' Park. Some other hitherto unknown teams also appeared on the half-time score lists – including 'Derby City' more than once.

An updated scoreboard was installed in 1988 with assistance from NEI, remaining in place until ground redevelopment reached that end in the close season of 1993.

The dot matrix type display of this scoreboard lent itself to more fanciful output, including some barely recognisable facial portraits of Newcastle players. Strangely, a large number of these belonged to players who barely featured for the club (eg John Robertson), while the Mick Quinn image was surely scanned from a photo of so-called TV entertainer Bob Carolgees.

At other times random messages would flash across the scoreboard with only the vaguest connection to on-pitch events – Jim Smith's side being routinely welcomed with 'the Eagle has landed', while sub-standard loan signing Dave Mitchell's only goal for the club was greeted by 'that's the magic of Mitchell'.

For the punters in the crowd, occasional 'big race' results were displayed – once with disastrous consequences. The 1989 Grand National was staged on Saturday April 8th, which coincided with Newcastle hosting Aston Villa. An on-screen announcement duly confirmed the winning horse as 'Liverpool Bear'. Cue widespread grumbling and the disposing of apparently-worthless betting slips – with nobody seeming to have backed this hitherto unheard-of outsider (a real dark horse?) Unfortunately, it later came to light that a communication breakdown had resulted in the scoreboard operator mishearing the name of the actual winning horse, 'Little Polveir'.

The question of reinstalling a smaller scoreboard has often cropped up in recent years – with the stadium redevelopment ruling out the jumbo efforts seen elsewhere. To date there have been no developments in this area, save for the appearance of electronic countdown clocks at pitchside in July 2007.

— ALL THERE IN BLACK AND WHITE PART I —

A selection of vintage Magpie-related headlines from the written press:

'NORTH TRIUMPHS'

A slightly patronising *Daily Mirror* headline on the Monday following Newcastle United's 2–1 FA Cup Final success over Arsenal in April 1932.

'MILBURN A J.E.T'
The *Sunday Pictorial* created a suitable headline for their reporting of Newcastle United's 2–0 1951 FA Cup Final victory over Blackpool from the initials of the scorer's name.

'IT'S OURS'
Accompanying a report of the cup win, telephoned direct from the Empire Stadium by Stan Bell and published in the *Evening Chronicle*, 1951.

'IT'S OURS AGAIN!'
The obvious accompaniment to news of the 1952 Wembley trophy success. However, the *Evening Chronicle* actually kept this one under wraps until the 3–1 final victory over Manchester City in 1955 (the 1952 headline was "United Bring Home the Cup Again").

'HUGHIE OF THE MAGIC FEET IS DEAD'
The *Newcastle Journal* headline in June 1957, following the discovery of the body of former Magpie legend Hughie Gallacher, who had taken his own life by standing in front of a train.

'HARVEY BRAVES RIP TO EUROPE GLORY'
Confirmation of Newcastle United's Fairs Cup success in 1969 in the *Daily Mirror*.

'SALUTE SUPERMAC'
Tyneside's new hero celebrates his home debut with a hat-trick over Liverpool in August 1971, reports the *Daily Mirror*.

'GORDON WHO?'
The *Newcastle Evening Chronicle* back page headline that greeted new manager Gordon Lee in June 1975. The quote came from United striker Malcolm Macdonald, who was in South Africa when Tyneside journalist John Gibson broke the news to him.

— NOT SO SAFE HANDS —

Outfield players who have gone between the posts for Newcastle in competitive matches include:

Player	Year	Fixture	Comp	Score
John King	1915	Tottenham Hotspur (a)	League	0–0
Bobby Moncur	1970	Manchester United (h)	League	5–1
Chris Waddle	1983	Leeds United (a)	League	1–0
Chris Hedworth	1986	West Ham United (a)	League	1–8
Peter Beardsley	1986	West Ham United (a)	League	1–8
Kevin Brock	1992	Birmingham City (a)	League	3–2

The Hedworth/Beardsley appearances took place in one amazing night at the Boleyn Ground in April 1986. Newcastle had taken to the field with a clearly unfit Martin Thomas between the posts and reserve keeper Dave McKellar sidelined with a hip injury.

After Thomas had further damaged his injured shoulder and conceded four goals, he was replaced by Ian Stewart at the interval with 22-year-old defender Chris Hedworth going in goal on what was only his tenth (and final) appearance for the club.

Hedworth was then also injured whilst challenging Tony Cottee as the West Ham striker scored the fifth goal and also had to be withdrawn, reducing the Magpies to ten men.

Peter Beardsley then took over goalkeeping duties and won the applause of the crowd with some good stops, but ultimately conceded three goals – and left his manager, former Newcastle keeper Willie McFaul calling this the most bizarre game of his career.

West Ham defender Alvin Martin scored a remarkable hat-trick in this game – netting once past each of the three 'keepers. Meanwhile, future Newcastle and West Ham manager Glenn Roeder didn't help the visitors' cause by scoring an own goal.

— IT'S ALL BALLS —

The first time that Newcastle supporters – or at least those with access to a wireless – were able to hear the FA Cup draw 'live' was when the BBC broadcast the third round draw on 16th December 1935.

On that occasion, the Magpies were handed a trip to the Anlaby Road ground of Hull City – a tie that they won 5–1.

It is recorded that the FA Secretary Stanley Rous was requested that day "to ensure that the bag is shaken for a few seconds to produce a distinctive and suitable sound".

— WEST SIDE STORY —

Now home to a towering construction boasting 15,000 seats and corporate facilities for half that number, the present Milburn Stand is built on the site of the smaller West Stand. Designed by Glaswegian architect Alexander Blair and opened in September 1905 for a 2–2 draw with Manchester City, the 4,655-seater stand itself replaced earlier less solid erections that had existed since 1897 – with the pitch re-sited a few yards further away from Leazes Terrace.

Constructed by Dunston-based firm Isaac Bewley, the stand included a swimming pool, billiard room and gym plus a curved central section housing the press box. Standing terraces were positioned in front of the seating deck – of which the Centre Pavilion was the Victorian equivalent of the Platinum Club.

The following 82 years saw only minor alterations to the West Stand, with a new entrance facing Barrack Road added in 1956. The much-recalled NEWCASTLE UNITED FC painted lettering on the rear appeared in the late 1960s, at which point the overall colour of the stand altered from the original off-white to a darker grey.

Following an investigation into the Bradford City fire of 1985, the need for a replacement stand became pressing, with the removal of the hated fences and installation of emergency exits from the seats onto the paddocks allowing a safety certificate to be issued. The distinctive "crows nest" press box was also closed on safety grounds, access only possible via a spiral staircase leading into the stand.

Its wooden construction meant that a noise akin to the rumble of thunder could be generated at times of high excitement by thousands of pairs of feet stamping on the floor. The starlings that used to plague the city in great numbers, meanwhile, roosted at nightfall amid great squawking, while the smell of the hops from the nearby Tyne Brewery was ever-present.

The end finally came in summer 1987 when the bulldozers moved in to the West Stand and the following season saw the teams hosed in portakabin dressing rooms at the North East corner.

Costing £5.5m and labelled The Peter Beardsley Stand by malcontents (on the basis that the player's move to Liverpool was alleged to have helped the club fund this redevelopment), this 6,607-seater stand took shape during 1987 before the first sections were opened the following year. Christened the Milburn Stand in honour of the recently deceased former Magpie hero, his widow Laura performed the official naming ceremony before a game against Ipswich Town.

The stand would survive less than a decade in its original form, however, with a radical rebuilding programme seeing new Leazes and Gallowgate Stands joined to the Milburn Stand in 1995 to form a continuous roof around the stadium – and the previous standing paddocks converted to seating.

Barely three years later, though, it was all change again, as plans to uplift the capacity of SJP from the routinely sold-out 36,000 to over 50,000 were given the green light in 1998. It took until August 2000 for the towering new structure to be opened and the cranes that had become a familiar feature on the skyline to be dismantled.

A complex operation to a graft an additional tier on the existing stand using some 7,200 tonnes of steel was carried out while the ground remained open, with temporary floodlights and pillars causing some inconvenience to fans – and rain jackets issued to those occupying roofless areas of seating.

Since then, cosmetic changes to the seating deck have included the enlargement of the Directors' Box and corporate areas, plus the repositioning of the press box to pitch level.

— CAN WE PLAY YOU EVERY WEEK? —

Opposition	Frequency	Record	Pts
Aston Villa	18 visits	12 wins, 4 draws, 2 defeats	40
Everton	18 visits	11 wins, 4 draws, 3 defeats	37
Tottenham Hotspur	18 visits	10 wins, 5 draws, 3 defeats	35
West Ham United	15 visits	8 wins, 5 draws, 2 defeats	29
Southampton	12 visits	9 wins, 1 draw, 2 defeats	28
Liverpool	18 visits	8 wins, 4 draws, 6 defeats	28
Bolton Wanderers	12 visits	8 wins, 3 draws, 1 defeat	27
Middlesbrough	13 visits	7 wins, 5 draws, 1 defeat	26
Chelsea	18 visits	7 wins, 5 draws, 6 defeats	26
Arsenal	18 visits	5 wins, 8 draws, 5 defeats	23
Coventry City	8 visits	7 wins, 1 draw, 0 defeats	22
Blackburn Rovers	16 visits	6 wins, 4 draws, 6 defeats	22
Manchester City	13 visits	6 wins, 2 draws, 5 defeats	20
Leicester City	8 visits	6 wins, 1 draw, 1 defeat	19
Leeds United	11 visits	5 wins, 3 draws, 3 defeats	18
Derby County	7 visits	5 wins, 2 draws, 0 defeats	17
Manchester United	18 visits	4 wins, 5 draws, 9 defeats	17
Sheffield Wednesday	7 visits	5 wins, 1 draw, 1 defeat	16

Wimbledon	7 visits	5 wins, 1 draw, 1 defeat	16
Sunderland	10 visits	4 wins, 4 draws, 2 defeats	16
Birmingham City	6 visits	5 wins, 0 draws, 1 defeat	15
Fulham	10 visits	4 wins, 3 draws, 3 defeats	15
Wigan Athletic	6 visits	4 wins, 2 draws, 0 defeats	14
West Bromwich Albion	6 visits	4 wins, 1 draws, 1 defeat	13
Charlton Athletic	8 visits	3 wins, 4 draws, 1 defeat	13
Nottingham Forest	4 visits	4 wins, 0 draws, 0 defeats	12
Portsmouth	6 visits	3 wins, 2 draws, 1 defeat	11
Norwich City	4 visits	3 wins, 1 draw, 0 defeats	10
Queens Park Rangers	4 visits	3 wins, 0 draws, 1 defeat	9
Ipswich Town	4 visits	2 wins, 2 draws, 0 defeats	8
Bradford City	2 visits	2 wins, 0 draws, 0 defeats	6
Reading	2 visits	2 wins, 0 draws, 0 defeats	6
Watford	2 visits	2 wins, 0 draws, 0 defeats	6
Wolves	3 visits	1 win, 2 draws, 0 defeats	5
Crystal Palace	3 visits	1 win, 1 draw, 1 defeat	4
Stoke City	3 visits	1 win, 1 draw, 1 defeat	4
Barnsley	1 visit	1 win, 0 draws, 0 defeats	3
Oldham Athletic	1 visit	1 win, 0 draws, 0 defeats	3
Sheffield United	2 visits	1 win, 0 draws, 1 defeat	3
Swindon Town	1 visit	1 win, 0 draws, 0 defeats	3
Swansea City	1 visit	0 wins, 1 draw, 0 defeats	1
Blackpool	1 visit	0 wins, 0 draws, 1 defeat	0
Hull City	1 visit	0 wins, 0 draws, 1 defeat	0

— MIND GAMES —

April 29th 1996. Newcastle have just won 1–0 at Elland Road against Leeds United and Kevin Keegan is interviewed live on Sky Sports:

Kevin Keegan: "I think you've got to send Alex Ferguson a tape of this game, haven't you? Isn't that what he asked for?"

Andy Gray (Sky pundit): "Well I'm sure if he was watching it tonight, Kevin, he could have no arguments about the way Leeds went about their job and really tested your team."

Kevin Keegan: "And . . . and . . . we . . . we're playing Notts Forest on Thursday and . . . he objected to that! Now that was fixed up four months ago. We f . . . supposed to play Notts Forest. I mean that sort of stuff, we . . . is it's been . . . we're bet, we're bigger than that."

Richard Keys (Sky Anchorman): "But that's part and parcel of the psychology of the game, Kevin, isn't it?"

Andy Gray: "No, I don't think so."

Kevin Keegan: "No! When you do that, with footballers, like he said about Leeds. And when you do things like that about a man like Stuart Pearce . . . I've kept really quiet, but I'll tell you something, he went down in my estimation when he said that.

"But I'll tell ya – you can tell him now if you're watching it – we're still fighting for this title and he's got to go to Middlesbrough and get something, and I tell you honestly, I will l love it if we beat them . . . love it!"

Richard Keys: "Well, quite plainly the message is, it's a long way from over and you're still in there scrapping and battling and you'll take any of these just as long as you continue to get the results?"

Kevin Keegan: "I think football in this country is so honest and so . . . honestly, when you look sometimes abroad, you've got your doubts. But it really has got to me and I, I, I've not voiced it live, not in front of the press or anywhere – I'm not even going to the Press Conference. But the battle's still on and Man United have not won this yet!"

While the 'love it' segment is routinely used to illustrate Keegan's misplacement of the plot, the full text tells a different story.

Keegan's reference to Pearce stemmed from Newcastle agreeing to participate in the Nottingham Forest defender's testimonial – eight days after the two sides were due to meet in a Premier League fixture.

Alex Ferguson then publicly claimed Forest would go easy on Newcastle because of Pearce's influence and that Leeds would similarly slacken off against Keegan due to their hatred of the Red Devils.

In the event Newcastle's title bid crumbled in a 1–1 draw at Forest, while the one team which lied down and died proved to be former United star Bryan Robson's Middlesbrough – allowing Manchester United the freedom of the Riverside on the final day of the season, the Red Devils claiming the title after a 3–0 victory on Teesside.

— THE FINAL COUNTDOWN, OR NOT? —

Opinion remains divided over whether the everyday phrase 'back to square one' can be attributed to the first live radio commentaries of sporting events – including one featuring Newcastle United.

The development of portable broadcasting equipment persuaded the BBC to venture into sports events, with a successful experiment to transmit live radio commentary from the England versus Wales rugby union fixture at Twickenham in January 1927. To coincide with this event, the BBC published a diagram of the playing surface divided into eight equal, numbered sections in that week's *Radio Times*. Then as the commentator broadcast news of the play, a second voice solemnly intoned the square number where the action was taking place.

Judged a success, the enterprise decamped to Highbury the following week, where coverage of the Arsenal versus Sheffield United fixture was broadcast, with a similar grid again being published.

Seven days later the BBC broke further new ground by transmitting their first-ever FA Cup tie. The game chosen was the fourth round match between First Division leaders Newcastle United and the renowned amateur side Corinthians – who had only compromised on their principles of non-competitiveness in order to participate in the FA Cup for the first time in 1922.

With the BBC's commentator Captain Henry Blythe Thornhill 'Teddy' Wakelam at the microphone, wireless set owners (with their *Radio Times* grids at the ready) and 56,338 supporters at the Crystal Palace ground in Sydenham heard and saw United end their winless run at this venue with a 3–1 success.

It has long been claimed that the act of the ball moving into the first square on the grid, in other words right back to one end of the pitch, gave rise to the popular phrase 'back to square one'. However, doubt was cast on the tale by the BBC themselves, in an edition of the TV programme *Balderdash and Piffle* in 2006. This questioned the fact that the phrase was in general use before World War II, disputing whether the actual phrase was ever uttered as part of the grid commentary.

— BLACK AND WHITE AND READ ALL OVER —

Saturday December 17th 2005 saw the final curtain fall on a Tyneside sporting institution, when the final edition of the *Pink* rolled off the printing presses at Thomson House.

A dedicated sports newspaper that had been produced by the *Evening Chronicle* for 110 years under various titles, with an (almost) kick-by-kick report of Newcastle's game that afternoon painstakingly rung in from the ground and recorded by copytakers.

Along with results (and later scorers) from the rest of the Football League and that all-important pools information, the whole thing was somehow bundled together, printed and distributed across the region by early evening.

The advent of mobile phone technology and text messaging however ultimately saw sales drop to an unacceptable level. The mortal blow though was the growth of Sky TV – bringing scores instantly into pubs and homes, while also ending the tradition of Saturday afternoon games.

Various attempts to provide alternative content in the *Pink* were made, but ultimately Newcastle's dominance of Sunday live schedules was to provide decisive. Gimmicks like making the publication date Saturday and Sunday just didn't work.

While the coverage of grassroots football, rugby and other minority sports such as speedway attracted some devotees, too few readers were prepared to fork out the increasing cover price on a non-match day, even if Sunderland had lost.

Prior to the 1963/64 season the paper was produced on normal newsprint, but a 3–1 home victory over Derby County on August 24th 1963 was the subject matter of the first 'Sports Edition' to be printed on the distinctive pink paper (although the title didn't change for a number of years).

At least the last-ever edition was able to report on a significant success – that of a 4–2 victory at West Ham for Newcastle, featuring a Michael Owen hat-trick.

The *Pink* name lives on in cyberspace, with post-match reports appearing under that banner on the icnewcastle website.

Some classic *Pink* headlines:

Aug 1971	'Mac Cracks In Super Three'	Newcastle United 3 Liverpool 2
Aug 1982*	'Kev's Big Day a Hit'	Newcastle United 1 QPR 0
Jan 1990	'Cloud Nine'	Newcastle United 5 Leicester City 4
Feb 1992**	'It's A Kracker'	Newcastle United 3 Bristol City 0
May 1992	'Safe!'	Leicester City 1 Newcastle United 2
Apr 1999	'Four-midable'	Derby County 3 Newcastle United 4
Feb 2000	'Red and Buried'	Newcastle United 3 Manchester Utd 0

Sep 2002	'Toons of Glory'	Newcastle United 2
		Sunderland 0
Apr 2005+	'Disgrace'	Newcastle United 0
		Aston Villa 3
Dec 2005	'Owe Yes!'	West Ham United 2
		Newcastle United 4

* Kevin Keegan's playing debut for the club.

** Kevin Keegan's managerial debut for the club.

+ Lee Bowyer and Kieron Dyer sent off for fighting with each other.

— FLYING THE FLAG PART II —

In addition to the overseas tours involving Newcastle United players organised by the English FA over the years, their counterparts at the Northern Irish FA also mounted similar tours – a ten-game stint in North America during May and June 1953 involving Magpie duo Tommy Casey and Alf McMichael.

For Casey it was a first taste of international football some two years before his debut senior cap, while McMichael served his country with distinction between 1949 and 1960. The men in green didn't have things all their own way across the Atlantic, however, winning six out of seven games against regional Canadian representative XIs, but losing all three matches against touring European club sides.

Getting underway with a 4–0 reverse at the hands of Liverpool in Brooklyn after sailing into New York, the men from Anfield then ran out 3–1 winners in Montreal later in the tour. The excursion then concluded with a 4–1 loss to Swiss side Young Boys in Montreal.

Alf failed to get on the scoresheet at all during the tour, but Tommy netted twice in a 10–0 romp against Saskatchewan staged in the splendidly named town of Moose Jaw.

— TOON TALISMEN —

Newcastle United's top ten Premiership goalscorers:

Player	Total
Alan Shearer	148
Peter Beardsley	47
Andy Cole	43

Les Ferdinand	41
Shola Ameobi	40
Nolberto Solano	37
Robert Lee	34
Gary Speed	29
Obafemi Martins	28
Craig Bellamy	27

— TWO-TIME TOONS —

Players who enjoyed two separate spells on the books of Newcastle United include:

Player	First Spell	Second Spell
Peter Beardsley	1983–87	1993–97
John Burridge	1989–91	1993
Lee Clark	1989–97	2005–06
John Craggs	1964–71	1982–83
Bobby Cummings	1954–56	1963–65
Robbie Elliott	1991–97	2001–06
Robert Gibson	1911–12	1919–20
Mick Harford	1980–81	1982
Terry Hibbitt	1971–75	1978–81
George Luke	1950	1959–61
Terry McDermott	1973–74	1982–84
Mark McGhee	1977–79	1989–91
David Mills	1982	1983–84
George Nevin	1925	1928–30
Ken Prior	1952–54	1956–57
Jimmy Richardson	1928–34	1937–38
Nolberto Solano	1998–04	2005–07
Pavel Srnicek	1991–98	2006–07
Tommy Wright	1988–93	1999

The shortest return was undoubtedly that of striker Mick Harford, who rejoined Newcastle on a free transfer from Bristol City after the Ashton Gate side defaulted on their payments, before immediately being sold on to Birmingham City.

A number of other players have subsequently returned to serve at St James' Park in an off-field capacity, including managerial trio Joe Harvey, Kevin Keegan and Glenn Roeder.

Inside-right Charlie Woods can claim the longest gap between stints at Newcastle. Transferred from Newcastle to Bournemouth and Boscombe Athletic in 1962, Woods returned as part of Sir Bobby Robson's backroom team in 2000 – a period of just under 38 years.

— BOER BORE —

Of particular note among Newcastle's many pre- and post-season tours was the 1952 jaunt to Southern Africa, when the FA Cup holders were accompanied by the trophy, thanks to a special licence being granted for it to be taken out of Great Britain.

In total, the tour took 70 days to complete, with the party travelling over 21,000 miles in the process. No fewer than 16 friendly matches were played, with Newcastle scoring 73 goals in the process.

Newcastle travelled with 16 players: Ron Batty, Frank Brennan, Bobby Cowell, Charlie Crowe, Reg Davies, Bill Foulkes, George Hannah, Joe Harvey, Jackie Milburn, Bobby Mitchell, Alf McMichael, Ted Robledo, George Robledo, Ronnie Simpson, Bob Stokoe and Tommy Walker.

Both George Robledo and Jackie Milburn picked up injuries in the early games which restricted their involvement (Milburn played just five times) and forced trainer Norman Smith to play defender Frank Brennan in an unfamiliar forward role.

The best individual scoring performance came in the Border Province fixture, when George Robledo weighed in with seven of the ten goals scored.

When questioned by reporters when the party eventually arrived back in England, captain Joe Harvey was scathing in his criticism of the tour itinerary, saying: "The unending travelling, the hard grounds and the atmospheric conditions were ordeals and I, for one, am glad it's all over. We should have played fewer games and we should have made Johannesburg the base instead of being hawked around South Africa non-stop."

Date	Opposition	Result
17th May	Southern Transvaal	won 3–2
21st May	Natal	won 6–2
24th May	Natal	won 4–0
31st May	Western Province	won 8–0
4th June	Griqualand West	won 3–0
7th June	Northern Transvaal	won 2–1

10th June	Lourenco Marques	won 5–0
14th June	Northern Rhodesia	won 6–1
18th June	Southern Rhodesia	won 4–2
21st June	East Transvaal	won 2–0
25th June	Orange Free State	won 3–0
28th June	South Africa	won 3–0 (in Durban)
2nd July	Border Province	won 10–0
5th July	Eastern Province	won 5–1
12th July	South Africa	lost 3–5 (in Johannesburg)
16th July	Southern Transvaal	won 6–4

— MAKING AN IMPRESSION —

Served by a dedicated station on the Metro light rail transit system since November 14th 1982, St James (without an apostrophe) was given a Toon Army-themed cosmetic facelift in the late 1990s.

Starting from street level, black-and-white portraits of past players are displayed on wall panels, while the surfaces above the escalators down to platform level feature blown-up photos of Newcastle supporters in full voice at Wembley Stadium. The usual yellow-and-cream interior station signage is replaced by black-and-white versions throughout.

To date, ten former Magpies have been commemorated on a "Walk of Fame" on the concourse, appropriately marked out as a football pitch; the grass effect achieved via green floor tiles.

Six outfield players have made boot casts, while three goalkeepers supplied hand prints and Manager Sir Bobby Robson trod on the concrete in his shoes:

May 17th 2001 Alan Shearer (boots)
May 17th 2001 Bobby Robson (shoes)
January 28th 2002 Peter Beardsley (boots)
May 15th 2002 Bob Moncur (boots)
June 2nd 2002 Malcolm Macdonald (boots)
December 5th 2002 Shay Given (hands)
September 18th 2003 Charlie Crowe (boots)
October 11th 2004 Philippe Albert (boots)
November 15th 2004 Iam McFaul (hands)
July 15th 2010 Steve Harper (hands)

At least two other Metro stations boast official Newcastle United-related artwork, with South Shields-born artist Bob Olley (famed for the "Westoe Netty" picture) incorporating some old boys on his "Famous Faces" mural at Monument.

Unveiled in 1996, the acrylic artwork features a Metro train with local celebrities as passengers, including Peter Beardsley (in his Newcastle shirt), Paul Gascoigne, former Chairman Sir John Hall and ex-Manager, Jack Charlton. The caricature of actor Robson Green is often mistaken for Alan Shearer – who was still a Blackburn Rovers player when the artwork was created.

Meanwhile, central on the network has been home to Hilary Paynter's installation "From the Rivers to the Sea" since 2004.

A series of wood engravings reproduced in monochrome on vitreous enamel panels, local urban and countryside scenes are depicted, including a view of the South Eastern corner of St James' Park.

— #9 DREAM PART II —

As well as the appearance ex-Toon striker Albert Stubbins on the cover of the *Sgt. Pepper . . .* album by the Beatles (see *#9 Dream Part I*, page 39) a second Magpies/Fab Four-related piece of artwork hit the shelves of the world's record shops during the 1970s.

On October 4th 1974 John Lennon's new album *Walls and Bridges* was released on the Apple/EMI label. While the music isn't remembered as vintage Lennon material despite the presence of guests such as Elton John, the cover artwork captured the work of Lennon the artist. The centrepiece of an intricate fold-out sleeve designed by Roy Kohara is a colour painting entitled 'Football' along with the legend 'John Lennon June 1952 age 11'.

That date and the clear depiction of players wearing the red and white of Arsenal and the black and white of Newcastle United confirm the subject of the painting to be a scene from 1952 FA Cup Final – which the Magpies won 1–0 at Wembley in May of that year.

And while the quality of the drawing is no better than the average 11-year-old would produce, it seems certain that the moment captured is the scoring of the only goal of the game, which came six minutes from full time.

In Lennon's picture, scorer George Robledo is seen tussling with Gunner's defender Lionel Smith in the air, with the ball just about to pass goalkeeper George Swindin en route to the Arsenal net. The whole scene is watched by a fourth player, Newcastle's number nine Jackie Milburn.

However, a November 2005 reissue of *Walls and Bridges* substituted this artwork for a photograph of Lennon taken by Bob Gruen.

— JOSSY'S GIANTS —

Written by TV darts commentator and fanatical Toon fan Sid Waddell, the TV show *Jossy's Giants* recounted the story of Jossy Blair, who after seeing his promising career as a Newcastle United player wrecked by injury, opened a sports shop ('Magpie Sports') and started coaching a junior football team.

Inevitably, the script called for a trip to St James' Park in an episode called 'The Promised Land' and Jossy and co. duly rolled up, to be met by Bobby Charlton and then-Magpies boss Willie McFaul, who guided them round the ground and onto the hallowed turf.

— INTERNATIONALISTS —

Newcastle United fielded a starting XI composed entirely of full internationals for the first time in their history against Everton at Goodison Park on Saturday February 28th 1998:

Player	Country
Shay Given	Republic of Ireland
Warren Barton	England
Steve Howey	England
Stuart Pearce	England
Philippe Albert	Belgium
David Batty	England
Robert Lee	England
Gary Speed	Wales
Alan Shearer	England
Andreas Andersson	Sweden
Keith Gillespie	Northern Ireland

Three of United's four unused replacements were also full internationals: Shaka Hislop (Trinidad & Tobago), John Barnes (England) and Jon Dahl Tomassson (Denmark). Only the selection of uncapped defender Darren Peacock prevented a full house.

— NEWCASTLE LEGENDS: JOE HARVEY —

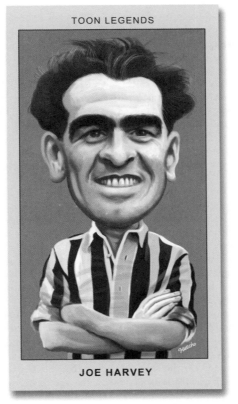

Joe Harvey: Honorary Geordie

Had Stan Seymour not been accorded the nickname 'Mister Newcastle', then Joe Harvey would have laid strong claim to it – like Seymour he served the club for many years as both captain and manager. As it is though, Harvey is one of a number of former Magpies deserving of the title of honorary Geordie – settling on Tyneside in preference to his native Yorkshire.

Spotted playing for Bradford City during World War II (when he scored twice against Newcastle), Harvey moved to St James' Park for £4,250 in October 1945.

He made his competitive debut for the club in 1946, in the same FA Cup tie against Barnsley as Jackie Milburn. Appointed captain, Harvey led by example on the field and had no problem making himself heard, having previously served as Company Sergeant-Major in the Royal Artillery.

A mainstay of the Newcastle side at right-half from 1946 to 1953 and a double FA Cup winner, Harvey then moved into the backroom staff before parting company with the club after the 1955 FA Cup Final to begin his managerial career.

He spent two years at Barrow, then moved the short distance to Workington, where he signed striker Ron McGarry, who was to follow Harvey when he returned to Tyneside as Newcastle manager in 1962.

Taking over a recently-relegated side which had flirted with a second relegation, Harvey rebuilt the team with new signings and graduates from the 1962 FA Youth Cup-winning side, eventually achieving promotion back to the First Division at the third attempt in 1964/65.

The summit of his footballing achievements came four years later when Newcastle brought European silverware back to Tyneside in 1969 – the second leg of the Inter-Cities Fairs Cup Final coinciding with Harvey's 51st birthday.

Having enjoyed Wembley success twice with the club on the field, defeat in the 1974 FA Cup Final against Liverpool proved to be a bitter blow and one from which Harvey never fully recovered, leaving his post within a year after some fans turned on him.

He remained on the staff at Gallowgate though, returning in a caretaker manager capacity in 1980 at the age of 62, while the club sought to appoint a replacement after sacking Bill McGarry.

Harvey died in February 1989, aged 70. His funeral, unlike Jackie Milburn's the previous year, was a low-key affair but nonetheless he remains firmly in the affections of generations of Newcastle supporters.

Joe Harvey factfile
Born: Edlington, November 6th 1918
Died: February 24th 1989
Newcastle career: 247 apps, 12 goals
Other clubs: Wolverhampton Wanderers, Bournemouth, Bradford

— FANTASY FOOTBALL —

Awarded since 1974, the Professional Footballer's Association have polled their own members on an annual basis to decide on a mythical Team of the Year in each of the top four divisions of English football.

Players selected by their peers while with Newcastle United were as follows:

1973/74	Malcolm Macdonald
1978/79	Peter Withe
1979/80	Peter Withe*
1982/83	Kevin Keegan*
1983/84	Kevin Keegan*
1984/85	Chris Waddle
1986/87	Peter Beardsley
1987/88	Paul Gascoigne
1989/90	Mick Quinn*
1992/93	John Beresford*/Lee Clark*/Gavin Peacock*
1993/94	Peter Beardsley
1995/96	Rob Lee/David Ginola/Les Ferdinand
1996/97	David Batty/Alan Shearer
1997/98	David Batty
2001/02	Shay Given
2002/03	Kieron Dyer/Alan Shearer
2005/06	Shay Given
2009/10	Jose Enrique*/Fabricio Coloccini*/Kevin Nolan*/Andy Carroll*
2011/12	Fabricio Coloccini

* selected in Division Two/Championship XI

PS: As of 2012, the most frequent nominee remains Kenny Sansom, who racked up 11 appearances between 1977 and 1987 while appearing for Crystal Palace and then Arsenal. That his contribution while at Newcastle United didn't warrant a 12th selection won't come as a shock to fans from that era . . .

— HOW YOU SAY, HOWAY? —

Players born outside the British Isles to have played first team football for Newcastle:

Player	Year signed	Country of birth
George Robledo	1949	Chile
Ted Robledo	1949	Chile
Arnold Woollard	1952	Bermuda
Preben Arentoft	1969	Denmark
Andy Parkinson	1978	South Africa
Frans Koenen	1980	Netherlands
Tony Cunningham	1985	Jamaica
Mirandinha	1987	Brazil
Bjorn Kristensen	1989	Denmark
Frank Pingel	1989	Denmark
Alan Neilson	1989	Germany
Pavel Srnicek	1990, 2006	Czech Republic
Nicky Papavasiliou	1993	Cyprus
Marc Hottiger	1994	Switzerland
Philippe Albert	1994	Belgium
David Ginola	1995	France
Faustino Asprilla	1996	Colombia
Jimmy Crawford	1997	USA
Alessandro Pistone	1997	Italy
Temuri Ketsbaia	1997	Georgia
Jon Dahl Tomasson	1997	Denmark
John Barnes	1997	Jamaica
Andreas Andersson	1998	Sweden
Nicos Dabizas	1998	Greece
Laurent Charvet	1998	France
Dietmar Hamann	1998	Germany
Nolberto Solano	1998, 2005	Peru
Stephane Guivarc'h	1998	France
George Georgiadis	1998	Greece
Didier Domi	1999	France
Louis Saha	1999	France
Silvio Maric	1999	Croatia
Marcelino	1999	Spain
Alain Goma	1999	France
Franck Dumas	1999	France
John Karelse	1999	Netherlands
Fumaca	1999	Brazil
Helder	1999	Angola
Diego Gavilan	2000	Paraguay
Daniel Cordone	2000	Argentina

Shola Ameobi	2000	Nigeria
Lomana Tresor Lua Lua	2000	DR Congo
Clarence Acuna	2000	Chile
Christian Bassedas	2000	Argentina
Olivier Bernard	2000	France
Laurent Robert	2001	Reunion Islands
Sylvain Distin	2001	France
Hugo Viana	2002	Portugal
Patrick Kluivert	2004	Netherlands
Charles N'Zogbia	2004	France
Ronny Johnsen	2004	Norway
Celestine Babayaro	2005	Nigeria
Jean-Alain Boumsong	2005	Cameroon
Amdy Faye	2005	Senegal
Emre	2005	Turkey
Tim Krul	2005	Netherlands
Albert Luque	2005	Spain
Craig Moore	2005	Australia
Matty Pattison	2006	South Africa
Obafemi Martins	2006	Nigeria
Giuseppe Rossi	2006	Italy
Antoine Sibierski	2006	France
David Edgar	2006	Canada
Oguchi Oneywu	2007	USA
David Rozehnal	2007	Czech Republic
Geremi	2007	Cameroon
Mark Viduka	2007	Australia
Claudio Cacapa	2007	Brazil
Habib Beye	2007	France
Tamas Kadar	2007	Hungary
Abdoulaye Faye	2007	Senegal
Jose Enrique	2007	Spain
Kazenga LuaLua	2008	DR Congo
Lamine Diatta	2008	Senegal
Sebastian Bassong	2008	France
Fabricio Coloccini	2008	Argentina
Jonas Gutierrez	2008	Argentina
Xisco	2008	Spain
Ignacio Gonzalez	2008	Uruguay
Peter Lovenkrands	2009	Denmark
Haris Vuckic	2009	Slovenia

Zurab Khizanishvili	2009	Georgia
Fabrice Pancrate	2009	France
Patrick Van Aanholt	2010	Netherlands
Cheick Tiote	2010	Ivory Coast
Hatem Ben Arfa	2010	France
Shefki Kuqi	2011	Yugoslavia
Yohan Cabaye	2011	France
Demba Ba	2011	France
Sylvain Marveaux	2011	France
Mehdi Abeid	2011	France
Gabriel Obertan	2011	France
Davide Santon	2011	Italy
Papiss Demba Cissé	2012	Senegal

— CHAIRMEN OF THE BOARD —

The men who have held the power at St James' Park:

Chairman	Appointed
Alex Turnbull	1892
D McPherson	1893
John Cameron	1894
William Nesham	1895
James Telford	1901
John Cameron	1904
Joseph Bell	1908
James Lunn	1909
George T Milne	1911
George G Archibald	1913
John Graham	1915
John P Oliver	1919
David Crawford	1928
James Lunn	1929
George F Rutherford	1941
John W Lee	1949
Robert Rutherford	1951
Stan Seymour	1953
Wilf Taylor	1955
William McKeag	1958
Wallace E Hurford	1959
William Westwood	1964

Robert J Rutherford	1978
Stan Seymour Junior	1981
Gordon McKeag	1988
George Forbes	1990
Sir John Hall	1991
Freddy Shepherd	1996
Sir John Hall	1998
Freddy Shepherd	1998
Chris Mort	2007
Derek Llambias	2008 (job title of Managing Director)

— NEWCASTLE LEGENDS: BOBBY MONCUR —

TOON LEGENDS

BOB MONCUR

Bobby Moncur: Desperate to lose the title
'last Newcastle captain to lift a major trophy'

No major cup tie featuring Newcastle would be complete without Bobby Moncur pleading for the current wearer of the armband to unseat him from his position as the last captain to lift a trophy for the club.

113

Since that balmy night in Budapest in 1969 when Moncur accepted the Fairs Cup from Sir Stanley Rous, no Toon skipper has come close to lifting further meaningful silverware.

The son of a policeman (who played centre half for the force), Perth-born Moncur came to the attention of Newcastle in 1960 as a 15-year-old playing for Scotland schoolboys. After summer trials that year with Preston North End, Wolverhampton Wanderers and Manchester United, Moncur turned down them all to sign for Newcastle.

Initially an inside-left, Moncur scored four times against West Wylam when guesting for the junior side and signed amateur forms before agreeing to put pen to paper as an apprentice for Charlie Mitten's squad in October 1960.

After rising through the junior and reserve sides and captaining the former to FA Youth Cup success in 1962, Moncur signed a full professional contract and made his debut as an 18-year-old away to Luton Town in March 1963. By then he was playing under Joe Harvey and had moved back into defence with some success, covering for injuries in the reserve side earlier that year. However, Moncur was to only feature sporadically for the first team, filling in at various times across the field. Such was his frustration at failing to gain a regular spot in the side that he asked to move on in 1967. Norwich City and Brighton and Hove Albion showed interest, but a move to the Canaries stalled when they were unwilling to meet Newcastle's £25,000 asking price.

After Newcastle's inconsistent start to the 1967/68 season, Moncur won a place in defence and impressed so much that he remained an ever-present, took the captain's armband from Frank Clark and ended the season with his first full Scotland cap. The following season he enhanced his reputation by leading Newcastle to Fairs Cup glory – although few could have predicted that his first three senior goals for the club would all come in the two-legged final against Hungary's Ujpesti Dozsa.

Moncur's final game in a black and white shirt came at Wembley against Liverpool in the 1974 FA Cup Final, before he left St James' Park for a two-year stint at Sunderland. Coaching and management jobs at Carlisle United (where he signed a young Peter Beardsley), Heart of Midlothian, Plymouth Argyle, Whitley Bay and Hartlepool United followed, before he ceased to be actively involved in the game in 1989.

Covering the club's fortunes for a time in the media, Moncur's association with Newcastle United continues with matchday hosting duties in a corporate suite named in his honour. A patron of the club's charitable foundation, he successfully battled colon cancer during 2008.

Bobby Moncur factfile
Born: Perth, January 19th 1945
Newcastle career: 361 apps, 10 goals
Other clubs: Sunderland, Carlisle United
International: Scotland, 16 apps, 0 goals

— MY GARDEN SHED . . . —

The 13,358 fans present at Selhurst Park on a Saturday in February 1994 have their part in history as the smallest crowd to have watched any of Newcastle's 692 Premier League games. They witnessed Wimbledon turn a 2–0 half-time lead into an eventual 4–2 success, with a brace of Peter Beardsley penalties all Kevin Keegan's Magpies had to show for their efforts on an afternoon when a visiting defence featuring Mike Hooper was unsettled by the presence of Vinnie Jones.

However, that was a good deal better than the record low turnout for a Premier League game just over a year earlier, when just 3,039 witnessed Everton's 3–0 humbling of a Wombles side managed by Joe Kinnear at the same venue.

The smallest crowds attending Newcastle games during each season of their Premier League participation have been:

1993/94	13,358	Wimbledon (Selhurst Park)
1994/95	14,203	Wimbledon (Selhurst Park)
1995/96	15,237	Southampton (The Dell)
1996/97	15,251	Southampton (The Dell)
1997/98	15,251	Southampton (The Dell)
1998/99	15,244	Southampton (The Dell)
1999/00	15,013	Southampton (The Dell)
2000/01	15,221	Southampton (The Dell)
2001/02	21,159	Fulham (Craven Cottage)
2002/03	17,900	Fulham (Loftus Road)
2003/04	16,506	Fulham (Loftus Road)
2004/05	19,003	Fulham
2005/06	20,220	Portsmouth (Fratton Park)
2006/07	19,225	Blackburn Rovers (Ewood Park)
2007/08	20,304	Wigan Athletic (JJB Stadium)
2008/09	19,416	Portsmouth (Fratton Park)
2010/11	15,277	Wigan Athletic (DW Stadium)
2011/12	16,211	Queens Park Rangers (Loftus Road)

— TEENAGE KICKS PART I —

Since taking their bow in the inaugural season of 1952/53, Newcastle United have captured the FA Youth Cup twice.

Season 1961/62 began with a resounding 14–0 success over Seaton Delaval, before amateur side Corinthians were defeated 3–0 on Tyneside. A 3–1 victory at Roker Park then led to a fourth round tie at Old Trafford against Manchester United – who had won the competition in the first five years it was staged. Goals from future first team players Bobby Moncur and Alan Suddick helped the young Magpies to a 2–1 victory. It's notable that at the time Moncur was playing in an advanced role and would only later revert to his more familiar defensive position.

A repeat of that scoreline then overcame local side North Shields and set up a two-legged semi-final against Portsmouth. The Magpies travelled to Hampshire by train and during the journey goalkeeper Stan Craig contrived to accidentally smash a carriage window and sit in the broken glass. He was able to play after having three stitches inserted in his backside, but couldn't stop Pompey from taking a one goal lead into the second leg.

A wet evening on Tyneside though saw United concede a further goal to trail by two at the interval. Some hope came from a Les O'Neil effort on 58 minutes, but with Pompey scoring again soon after, a first final appearance was only secured after a supreme effort. Goals from Matty Gowland, Les O'Neil again and a fine chip from George Watkin though won the day and set up a two-legged final against Wolverhampton Wanderers.

Nearly 14,000 fans were at Molineux to see the sides draw 1–1, with John Galley putting the Wolves ahead.

Clive Chapman then equalised with a memorable individual goal, dribbling past three opponents before beating Geordie-born goalkeeper Jim Barron. The return leg on Tyneside saw 20,588 in attendance at Gallowgate, Wolves seeing an effort chalked off before Bob Moncur decisively headed home a Les O'Neil corner at the near post just before the hour. Captain Colin Clish collected the cup.

A week later, Moncur signed his first professional contract with Newcastle United. The club were also billed £10 for the damage to the train window. Eight of the final side went on to feature in the Magpies first team: David Craig, Colin Clish, John Markie, Bobby Moncur, Les O'Neil, Alan Suddick, Dave Turner and George Watkin. The other three players were: Clive Chapman, Stan Craig and Matty

Gowland. Alan Wilkinson played in earlier rounds before being injured.

— LEAGUE CUP FINAL ONE-OFF —

Newcastle's sole League Cup final appearance came in February 1976, when Manchester City won 2–1 at Wembley thanks to goals from Peter Barnes and an acrobatic bicycle kick from Geordie Dennis Tueart. Alan Gowling had equalised in between for Newcastle, while future Magpies coach Willie Donachie wore the number 3 shirt for the victors.

The cup run began with a second round tie against Division Four side Southport that was switched from Haig Avenue to St James' Park in order to earn the Lancashire club extra revenue.

Bristol Rovers of Division Four were then beaten after a draw at Eastville and a replay on Tyneside, before Division One side QPR were overcome at Loftus Road for the second successive season in this competition.

A quarter-final tie with Second Division Notts County followed and despite Newcastle enjoying home advantage, the other Magpies proved to be tricky opponents until goalkeeper Eric McManus fumbled a long Macdonald throw into his own net.

A trip to Wembley was then secured after the team turned round a one-goal deficit from the first leg at White Hart Lane in a memorable home display against Tottenham Hotspur.

Manchester City, meanwhile, had overcome Norwich City, Nottingham Forest, Manchester United and Mansfield Town, and a Tyne-Tees final was avoided when Tony Book's side disposed of Jack Charlton's Middlesbrough at the semi-final stage.

The road to Wembley:

Round	Opponent	Score	Scorers
Second	Southport (h)	6–0	Gowling 4, Cannell 2
Third	Bristol Rovers (a)	1–1	Gowling
Third Replay	Bristol Rovers (h)	2–0	T. Craig (pen), Nattrass
Fourth	Queens Park Rangers (a)	3–1	Macdonald, Burns, Nulty
Fifth	Notts County (h)	1–0	McManus (og)
Semi-final (1)	Tottenham Hotspur (a)	0–1	

Semi-final (2)	Tottenham Hotspur (h)	3–1	Gowling, Keeley, Nulty
Final	Manchester City (n)	1–2	Gowling

— BACK TO THE FUTURE —

Future Newcastle players and managers who picked up FA Youth Cup honours earlier in their careers, include:

Year	Player	Playing for
1953	Albert Scanlon	Manchester United
1954	Albert Scanlon	Manchester United
1967	Colin Suggett	Sunderland
1970	Graeme Souness	Tottenham Hotspur
1970	Ray Clarke	Tottenham Hotspur
1973	Dave McKellar	Ipswich Town
1977	Kenny Sansom	Crystal Palace
1978	Kenny Sansom	Crystal Palace
1989	Jason Drysdale	Watford
1992	Nicky Butt	Manchester United
1993	Keith Gillespie	Manchester United
1996	Michael Owen	Liverpool
1997	Jonathan Woodgate	Leeds United

— NEUTRAL TERRITORY —

As well as being used as a venue for international matches over the years, St James' Park has hosted various competitive club fixtures not featuring Newcastle United:

Date	Result	Competition
April 18th 1903	Sunderland 2 Middlesbrough 1	Division One
December 23rd 1935	Hartlepool 4 Halifax Town 1	FA Cup replay
February 6th 1952	Gateshead 0 West Bromwich A 2	FA Cup replay
March 13th 1954	Bishop Auckland 5 Brigg Sports 1	FA Amateur Cup

April 19th 1954	Bishop Auckland 2 Crook Town 2	FA Amateur Cup
November 28th 1955	Carlisle United 1 Darlington 3	FA Cup replay
March 17th 1956	Bishop Auckland 5 Kingstonian 1	FA Amateur Cup
March 16th 1957	Bishop Auckland 2 Hayes 0	FA Amateur Cup
March 12th 1960	Crook Town 1 Kingstonian 2	FA Amateur Cup
March 28th 1964	Crook Town 2 Barnet 1	FA Amateur Cup
January 16th 1967	Middlesbrough 4 York City 1	FA Cup replay
March 18th 1972	Blyth Spartans 0 Enfield 0	FA Amateur Cup
February 27th 1978	Blyth Spartans 1 Wrexham 2	FA Cup replay --
September 3rd 1994	Gateshead 0 Yeovil Town 3	GM Vauxhall Conference
December 7th 1925	Blyth Spartans 1 Hartlepools United 1	FA Cup replay
November 19th 1928	Jarrow 2	FA Cup replay York City 3
November 25th 1946	Ashington 1	FA Cup replay North Shields 3

The Wear-Tees derby of April 1903 was played on Tyneside as a punishment for Sunderland, after their fans had stoned the motor coach carrying players of The Wednesday (later Sheffield Wednesday) on Wearside earlier that month.

The only other occasion when the stadium has been used for a league match not involving Newcastle came in 1994, when cross-Tyne neighbours Gateshead were unable to play at their usual home venue due to an athletics meeting taking place at the International Stadium. United allowed their fellow Tynesiders use of St James' Park, giving Yeovil fans among the 2,734 crowd their first – and so far only – opportunity to see the Glovers play at Gallowgate.

The appearance of the visitors was fitting, given that Newcastle had provided the opposition four years previously when Yeovil christened their new Huish Park ground.

— CAUGHT IN THE TRIANGLE —

Thanks to some underachievement in the FA Cup in January 1986, fourth round day arrived with Newcastle lacking a fixture. A 0–2 home reverse at the hands of Brighton had ended the Magpies' Wembley dreams for another year, while Brian Clough's Nottingham Forest were similarly underemployed – having lost to Blackburn Rovers in a replay.

A friendly match between the two stages was duly arranged – but in the slightly unexpected and thoroughly exotic venue of Bermuda.

Thanks to a sponsorship deal brokered with a Nottingham-based businessman, the two sides were flown out to the tropical island and faced each other at the Somerset Cricket Club ground in Sandys Parish.

The final score was a resounding 0–3 defeat at the hands of Forest, whose goals came from David Campbell (2) and Ian Bowyer.

Just over a fortnight later the two sides met again, this time in a Division One fixture. On that occasion, two Peter Beardsley goals gave Willie McFaul's side ample revenge at the City Ground – in rather chillier conditions.

That completed a hectic period for Beardsley, who had taken part in the Bermuda game before flying on to Egypt, linking up with the England squad and making his full international debut in Cairo.

— A QUESTION OF VEXILLOLOGY —

Some flag and banner-related stories:

- Reports of a riot that took place before the scheduled Tyne-Wear derby match of April 1901 mention that the club flag was torn down by rampaging Sunderland fans. Images of St James' Park at that time show a flag flying from the south-west corner of the stadium, but by the 1950s a large Union Jack flag can be seen fluttering from a flag pole at the South East corner.
- The same location also saw the so-called 'ten-minute flag' fly for some years – a large flag with black and white vertical stripes displayed throughout the match until taken down to indicate that the 80th minute had been reached.
- The club's revival in the 1990s then saw Newcastle supporters club together and buy a large flag. This was unfurled for the first

time in April 1992 from the East Stand, after victory over Sunderland virtually secured promotion. The horizontally-striped black and white flag read:

NEWCASTLE UNITED
TOON ARMY
CHAMPIONS 1992/93

- This flag became a familiar sight at games, being passed back and forward over the heads of fans. It made a belated comeback at Watford's Vicarage Road in the final game of the 2006/07 season.
- An even bigger flag measuring 120 feet by 80 feet then appeared in the 1993/94 season: another horizontal black and white effort emblazoned with a brewery blue star, two Magpie cartoon figures and the legend:

NEWCASTLE UNITED
HOWAY THE LADS

- This was also displayed within St James' Park but later labelled a fire risk and banned.
- After being draped from the partially-built Gallowgate Stand when Arsenal were beaten in May 1994, the flag then followed the club into Europe. Numerous appearances on the continent followed, including matches at Antwerp and Metz. However this second flag met its end during the November 1997 trip to Barcelona – failing to make it back from the rain-sodden Nou Camp.
- A third large flag did briefly appear in the 2004/05 season, complete with club badge. This was funded by Newcastle United and unfurled before the FA Cup semi-final tie with Manchester United at Cardiff's Millennium Stadium in April 2005. It also made brief appearances at St James' Park before home games in the following seasons.
- Alan Shearer's retirement in May 2006 was marked by a large banner showing him in familiar goalscoring celebration style and titled 'Thanks for Ten Great Years'. This was draped from the back of the Gallowgate Stand in the days leading up to his testimonial against Celtic.
- Unofficial flags and banners have appeared periodically over the years, with a "Sack the Board" banner much in evidence as the

121

club were demoted in 1989. And supporter discontent was clear during the relegation season 20 years later, with the appearance of the infamous "COCKNEY MAFIA OUT" banner at St James' Park.

- Another Shearer-related creation made the headlines in April 1998, when a giant replica 'Shearer 9' shirt briefly adorned the 'Angel of the North' sculpture. The mission to clothe Anthony Gormley's statue on the southern approaches to Tyneside was carried out by a group of supporters in the run up to the Wembley FA Cup final involving Newcastle and Arsenal. Fishing lines and catapults were used to hoist the 29 feet by 17 feet replica strip into place early one morning, although it was quickly lowered once the police became aware.

— TRIPLE CROWN —

The last time Newcastle competed in a League game for two points was on May 2nd 1981, when the Toon beat Orient 3–1 at St James' Park to complete an unmemorable eleventh-place finish in Division Two.

The following season three points were up for grabs for the first time when Watford were the opening day visitors to Tyneside. However, Newcastle went down 0–1 to the Hornets and were beaten 0–3 at Loftus Road by Queens Park Rangers the following week. It was only at the third attempt that a three point maximum was recorded, thanks to a 1–0 win over Cambridge United at St James' Park on September 12th 1981. The all-important goal came from midfielder John Trewick.

— STATUESQUE II —

In addition to the various Jackie Milburn statues (see Statuesque I), the North East now boasts a cast image of popular former Magpies Manager, Sir Bobby Robson.

Commissioned and funded by Newcastle United, the nine-foot image was made in bronze by local sculptor Tom Maley and positioned at the South West Corner of St James' Park. That's an appropriate site, given that Maley's sculpture of Jackie Milburn was previously displayed there.

Sir Bobby's widow Lady Elsie unveiled the statue in May 2012, having officially opened a nearby memorial garden to her late husband 12 months earlier – featuring five carved stones, each commemorating a memorable era of his life. And completing a trio of Robson-related tributes, Tom Maley's bronze bust of Sir Bobby is located in Old Milburn Reception.

Looking farther afield meanwhile, a trio of Magpie-related statues can be found outside stadia elsewhere in the United Kingdom.

Ipswich Town can lay claim to the first Bobby Robson statue, with the subject himself proudly unveiling a work by Sean Hedges-Quinn outside Portman Road in 2002. The same sculptor then saw his interpretation of former Newcastle player Bob Stokoe revealed in the shadow of Sunderland's Stadium of Light in 2006.

One of Stokoe's Magpie contemporaries was similarly commemorated the previous October, with the siting of statue Ivor Allchurch at Swansea City's Liberty Stadium.

Paid for by public subscription – including donations from Tyneside – a life-size representation of the "Golden Boy of Welsh Football" was cast in bronze by Michael Field.

PS: Statues of Tom Finney (Deepdale, Preston) and Stan Mortensen (Bloomfield Road, Blackpool) were unveiled in 2004 and 2005 respectively. Both appeared for Newcastle as guest players during World War Two. A statue of a third wartime guest, Bill Nicholson, is also planned by Tottenham Hotspur.

— MIND YOUR BACKS —

In 2012 it was the 90th anniversary of a dedicated tunnel linking the dressing rooms on the west side of St James' Park to the pitch without the need for pushing through the crowd, as was the case before 1922.

At that point two separate tunnels were constructed, before a single central access. Small shelters for home and visiting staff were later erected, remaining more or less untouched until the late 1980s, when enlarged facilities sprang up. The tunnel also gained a roof, replacing previous mesh wiring.

Further remodelling of the tunnel area followed conversion of the stadium to seating in the 1990s, with the roof removed to reveal steps up from the tunnel to pitch level – United opting not to follow the fad for concertina-type temporary tunnels.

Latterly though, the tunnel exterior has been covered once again, with a continuous roof extending across both dugouts.

— NEWCASTLE LEGENDS: JIMMY LAWRENCE —

TOON LEGENDS

JAMES LAWRENCE

Jimmy Lawrence: A great keeper, although the balls were a lot bigger in those days!

The statistics speak for themselves – record appearance maker, three First Division championship winners' medals, one FA Cup winner's medal and an unbroken 18-year spell on the books at Gallowgate.

Glaswegian keeper Jimmy Lawrence was signed by Newcastle in July 1904, taking the place of Charlie Watts between the posts in a 2–0 home win over Manchester City in October of that year.

A first championship medal followed that season, but so too did the first of four FA Cup Final defeats – two of which (in 1908 and 1911) came as a direct result of costly individual errors on Lawrence's part.

However, he was to pick up a winner's medal in 1910 against Barnsley – the first of two consecutive seasons when he appeared in FA Cup finals and replays.

Further championship-winning seasons followed in 1906/07 and 1908/09 – the latter being one of three seasons when Lawrence was an ever-present in both league and cup. And during his long Newcastle career, Lawrence boasted the enviable record of having saved four of the five penalty kicks he faced against Sunderland in Tyne-Wear derby fixtures.

Surprisingly for such a consistent performer he was only capped by Scotland once, in a Home International game against England in 1911 at Everton's Goodison Park.

Lawrence played his final game for Newcastle in April 1922 at home to Bradford City, before giving way to his successor Bill Bradley and moving on shortly after to become manager of Division Two side South Shields. A spell in charge of Preston North End followed, before he was persuaded to join German side Karlsruhe.

He enjoyed title success with the club in 1925, before returning to his native Scotland where he served Stranraer as both a director and chairman up until his death in 1934.

Jimmy Lawrence factfile
Born: Glasgow, February 16th 1885 Died: November 1934
Newcastle career: 496 apps (1904–21)
Other clubs: Partick Athletic, Hibernian, Newcastle United, South Shields (manager), Preston North End (manager), Karlsruhe (trainer), Stranraer (director and chairman)
International: Scotland, 1 cap

— GAP YEAR —

The sounding of the final whistle of the 2008/09 season was also the death knell for Newcastle's proud record of 17 consecutive Premier League campaigns. Uncertainty over the futures of both players and staff continued throughout that summer and a 1–6 loss to third-tier Leyton Orient in pre-season set alarm bells ringing. The air of gloom on Tyneside then deepened with the passing of Sir Bobby Robson less than two weeks before United kicked off their first season outside the top flight since 1992.

What unfolded over the following ten months, however, would restore the feel-good factor at St James' Park, as goals were scored, victories racked up and records began to tumble – all a far cry from pre-season fears of a second successive demotion.

Under the command of Chris Hughton, The Magpies captured the Championship, remained unbeaten on home soil all season and recorded a club record 22 clean sheets en route to the title. Scoring 90 goals (with Andy Carroll and Kevin Nolan joint top scorers with 17 apiece) was two less than Kevin Keegan's side of 1993, but the class of 2010 eclipsed them in various other ways:

1992/93 (46 game season) Won 29, Lost 8, Drawn 9.
92 goals scored, 38 conceded, 96 points, 1st place.

2009/10 (46 game season) Won 30, Lost 4, Drawn 12.
90 goals scored, 35 conceded, 102 points, 1st place.

The season concluded with a record-breaking 17 match unbeaten run, with promotion achieved on Easter Monday without kicking a ball thanks to a scoreless draw between Nottingham Forest and Cardiff City. Newcastle fans then invaded the pitch at Plymouth's Home Park two weeks later following a 2–0 victory that sealed the destination of the title.

Reflecting on United's successful return to the top flight at the first time of asking, Hughton was moved to say that:

". . . expectations maybe won't be as big as they have been in the past . . . I do think we need to bring players in but I don't see whole-sale changes."

Unfortunately for him, the club's decision-makers didn't share that view and dispensed with his services in December 2010, after 16 Premier League matches.

— SAFE HANDS . . . SOMETIMES —

During their 18 seasons of Premier League involvement, Newcastle have entrusted goalkeeping duties in their 692 league fixtures to just eight players:

Player	Year(s) played	Total	Subs
Shay Given	1997/2009	354	0
Steve Harper	1994/present	99	7
Pavel Srnicek	1993/1998, 2006/2007	97	2
Tim Krul	2010/present	58	1
Shaka Hislop	1995/1998	53	0
Mike Hooper	1993/1996	23	2
Tommy Wright	1993,1999	5	1
Jon Karelse	1993/2003	3	0

Meanwhile, another seven goalkeepers have taken their place on the substitutes' bench for the Magpies in the Premier League without being called into action:

John Burridge	1993
Tony Caig	2003/2006
Fraser Forster	2006/present
Peter Keen	1998/1999
Lionel Perez	1998/2000
Rob Elliot	2011/present
Ole Soderberg	2008/2012

Both Perez and Burridge played against Newcastle in the Premiership – for Sunderland and Manchester City respectively. Burridge kept a clean sheet in a 0–0 draw at Maine Road in April 1995 after appearing as a half-time replacement for Tony Coton. And as well as frustrating his former employers, who had released him six months earlier, that game saw him become the oldest player to appear in the Premiership, aged 43 years, four months and 26 days.

— ALL THERE IN BLACK AND WHITE PART II —

A selection of more recent Magpie-related headlines from the written press:

'KING KEVIN'

A suitable *Evening Chronicle* front page headline to accompany a photo of the Newcastle United manager Kevin Keegan wearing a crown, seconds after his side clinched promotion by winning at Grimsby Town in May 1993.

'HOT COLE'

Goal number 39 of the season for Magpies striker Andy Cole equalled the club's scoring record and helped United to a 2–0 victory over Liverpool at Anfield in 1994. *The Mirror* gauged the temperature nicely.

'HOWAY FIVE–0'

Surfing on a wave of mass hysteria on Tyneside, *The Sun* conjured up a classic headline to accompany their report of Newcastle United's 5–0 home success over Manchester United in October 1996.

'HO HO SEVEN'

It may have come three days after Christmas Day 1996, but Newcastle United's 7–1 home win over Tottenham Hotspur still prompted a seasonal effort from the *Sunday Mirror*.

'TEARS OF A TOON'

How *The Sun* reported reaction to the resignation of Kevin Keegan from the manager's job at Newcastle United, in January 1997.

'DREAM TEAM'

An epic night of European football on Tyneside in September 1997 ended with Barcelona on the wrong end of a Tino Asprilla treble.

'CLARKIE IN THE SHIRT'

News reached the *Sunday Sun* in June 1999 that then-Sunderland midfielder Lee Clark had been spotted at Wembley a month previously watching Newcastle United in the FA Cup Final. His attire for part of that day? A T-shirt with the slogan 'sad mackem b*stards'.

'SHEARER THRIVES WITH FIVE'

The *Guardian* documented the return to goalscoring form of striker Alan Shearer in September 1999, as Bobby Robson oversaw his first home game in charge at St James' Park. Final score: Newcastle United 8 Sheffield Wednesday 0 (Shearer 5).

'WOR MIKEY'
How the *Daily Mirror* announced the arrival of Michael Owen to Tyneside in August 2005.

'FINAL'
The *Evening Chronicle* reporting on the career-ending injury suffered by Alan Shearer during Newcastle's 4–1 victory on Wearside in April 2006.

— RING MASTERS —

With the return of a Great Britain team to the competition after a gap of 52 years, renewed attention was devoted to the Men's Olympic Football Tournament at the 2012 London Olympics. One then-current Magpie and various other former and future players have participated in the competition since it was first staged as part of the third Olympiad in 1904 as follows:

1920 Antwerp, Belgium:
Denmark: Jack Carr (Head Coach) First Round

1948 London, Great Britain:
Great Britain: Ronnie Simpson (Queens Park) Semi Finalist
Great Britain: Tom Curry (Assistant Coach) Semi Finalist
Egypt: Ike Keen (Head Coach) First Round
Netherlands: Jesse Carver (Head Coach) First Round

1988 Seoul, South Korea:
Australia: David Mitchell (Feyenoord) Quarter Finalist

1992 Barcelona, Spain:
Colombia: Faustino Asprilla (Atletico National) Group Stage

1996 Atlanta, USA:
Argentina: Christian Bassedas (Velez Sarsfield) Silver Medalist
Australia: Mark Viduka (Croatia Zagreb) Group Stage
France: Antoine Sibierski (Lille) Quarter Finalist
Italy: Alessandro Pistone (Inter Milan) Group Stage
Nigeria: Celestine Babayaro (Anderlecht) Gold Medalist

2000 Sydney, Australia:
Australia: Mark Viduka (Celtic) Group Stage
Cameroon: Geremi (Real Madrid) Gold Medalist
Nigeria: Celestine Babayaro (Chelsea) Quarter Finalist
Spain: Albert Luque (Real Mallorca) Silver Medalist

2004 Athens, Greece:
Argentina: Fabricio Coloccini (AC Milan) Gold Medalist
Australia: Craig Moore (Rangers) Quarter Finalist
Portugal: Hugo Viana (Newcastle United) Group Stage

2008 Beijing, China:
Australia: Craig Moore (Brisbane Roar) Group stage
Australia: James Troisi (unattached) Group stage
Italy: Giuseppe Rossi (Villarreal) Quarter Finalist

2012 London, Great Britain:
Great Britain: Stuart Pearce (Head Coach)

United youngster Mehdi Abeid appeared for Algeria in a pre-qualifying tournament staged in Morocco during 2011, but his side failed to land a place in the Finals.

— MEET THE MANAGERS —

Manager	Years in charge
Frank Watt	1895–1930 (secretary)
Andy Cunningham	1930–1935
Tom Mather	1935–1939
Stan Seymour	1939–1947 (honorary)
George Martin	1947–1950
Stan Seymour	1950–1954 (honorary)
Duggie Livingstone	1954–1956
Charlie Mitten	1958–1961
Norman Smith	1961–1962
Joe Harvey	1962–1975
Gordon Lee	1975–1977
Richard Dinnis	1977
Willie McFaul	1977 (caretaker)
Bill McGarry	1977–1980
Joe Harvey	1980 (caretaker)
Arthur Cox	1980–1984

Jack Charlton	1984–1985
Willie McFaul	1985–1988
Colin Suggett	1988 (caretaker)
Jim Smith	1988–1991
Bobby Saxton	1991 (caretaker)
Ossie Ardiles	1991–1992
Kevin Keegan	1992–1997
Terry McDermott*	1997 (caretaker)
Kenny Dalglish	1997–1998
Tommy Craig**	1998 (caretaker)
Ruud Gullit	1998–1999
Steve Clarke	1999 (caretaker)
Sir Bobby Robson	1999–2004
John Carver	2004 (caretaker)
Graeme Souness	2004 –2006
Glenn Roeder	2006–2007
Nigel Pearson****	2007 (caretaker)
Sam Allardyce	2007–2008
Nigel Pearson	2008 (caretaker)
Kevin Keegan	2008
Chris Hughton	2008 (caretaker)
Joe Kinnear	2008
Chris Hughton	2009 (caretaker)****
Alan Shearer	2009
Chris Hughton	2009–2010
Alan Pardew	2010–present

(* assisted by Arthur Cox)
(** assisted by Alan Irvine)
(*** assisted by Lee Clark)
(*** assisted by Colin Calderwood)

Note: Frank Watt guided the club from its inception, but the side was selected by a committee during this period. Stan Seymour, meanwhile, performed the duties of team manager in two separate periods, although player selection was again officially performed by a committee composed of himself and other club directors.

— GROWING PAINS —

Apart from their two successes in the FA Youth Cup, the Magpies have made six more losing appearances in the semi-finals:

Season	Opponent	Score/aggregate
1975/76	Wolverhampton Wanderers	lost 2–4 (1–2, 1–2)
1988/89	Manchester City	lost 1–3 (1–2, 0–1)
1998/99	Coventry City	lost 2–5 (0–4, 2–1)
2005/06	Manchester City	lost 3–4 (2–3, 1–1)
2006/07	Liverpool	lost 3–7 (2–4, 1–3)
2009/10	Aston Villa	lost 1–2 (1–1, 0–1)

— CUP MARATHONS —

Now that FA Cup games are settled after a single replay, extra time or penalties if necessary, it's easy to forget that until comparatively recently, ties were played to a finish – regardless of how many games that required.

The Magpies have required three games to settle a tie on five occasions, while they've twice embarked on four-game marathons. The first of these came in the 1923/24 season, when they were drawn away to lower league Derby County in the second round. A record attendance of 27,873 attended the Baseball Ground for the first game, which ended 2–2 after the Rams recovered from being two goals behind.

The replay took place on a Wednesday afternoon in front of 50,393 fans at St James' Park and again the Magpies took a 2–0 lead only to be pegged back to 2–2 once more – Derby's cause aided by an own goal from Ted Mooney.

With extra time failing to separate the teams, a third game at a neutral ground was required and this was eventually staged at Bolton's Burnden Park after much discussion.

The following Monday afternoon 17,300 fans saw Newcastle grab an equaliser in the dying seconds of extra time for a third consecutive 2–2 draw. Derby were incensed at some alleged favouritism from referee Sam Rothwell, who awarded a dubious penalty and free-kick – both of which United converted.

After further arguments between the sides failed to reach an agreement over the venue for a fourth game, a coin was tossed and Newcastle won the right to stage the tie on Tyneside 48 hours later – with a replacement referee.

A classic encounter at St James' Park saw the Magpies come back from two goals down, a Neil Harris hat-trick providing the platform for an eventual 5–3 win in front of 32,496 spectators.

A rather less incident-packed quartet of matches in season 1988/89 saw Newcastle eventually succumb to lower league Watford in round three.

After a goalless stalemate on Tyneside the teams re-convened at Vicarage Road two nights later, United recovering from conceding an early goal to force a 2–2 draw.

The following Monday it was scoreless against at St James' Park and 48 hours later neither side could break the deadlock back in Hertfordshire.

Finally, a goal came late in extra time with an unprecedented fifth match looking inevitable, a harmless shot being deflected into his own goal by Newcastle's Glenn Roeder (who was to play and manage both sides).

The tie lasted 450 minutes – 30 more than the one with Derby County – and was an unwanted burden as Jim Smith's side struggled unsuccessfully to avoid relegation.

— PLEASE BE UPSTANDING FOR... —

Full internationals staged at St James' Park:

Mar 18th 1901 England 6 (Bloomer 4, Needham, Foster) Wales 0 (HI)
Apr 6th 1907   England 1 (Bloomer) Scotland 1 (Compton OG) (HI)
Nov 15th 1933 England 1 (Brook) Wales 2 (Mills, Astley) (HI)
Nov 9th 1938   England 4 (Smith 2, Dix, Lawton) Norway 0 (FR)
Jun 10th 1996 France 1 (Dugarry) Romania 0 (ECF)
Jun 13th 1996 Bulgaria 1 (Stoichkov) Romania 0 (ECF)
Jun 18th 1996 France 3 (Blanc, Penev OG, Loko)
               Bulgaria 1 (Stoichkov) (ECF)
Sep 5th 2001   England 2 (Owen, Fowler) Albania 0 (ECF)
Aug 18th 2004 England 3 (Beckham, Owen, Wright-Phillips)
               Ukraine 0 (FR)

(HI=Home International, FR-Friendly, ECF=European Championship Finals, WCQ=World Cup Qualifier)

Newcastle United custodian Matt Kingsley was in the England lineup in 1901, with both Colin Veitch and John Rutherford followed suit six years later and John Wright appearing in 1938. England's 2004 visit featured a trio of then-current Magpie midfielders, Nicky Butt, Kieron Dyer and Jermaine Jenas appearing at various times.

— NEWCASTLE LEGENDS: KEVIN KEEGAN —

Kevin Keegan: Never a dull moment

When Kevin Keegan arrived at St James' Park in August 1982, the effect he had on a club languishing in the wastelands of Division Two was instant. Amid a media frenzy, fans queued across the car park to buy season tickets and suddenly the club was alive again.

England manager Bobby Robson attended his debut, a sell-out crowd of 36,000 delighting in a 1–0 win over Queens Park Rangers thanks to a Keegan goal. Just three months earlier, by comparison, fewer than 11,000 fans had seen Rangers triumph 4–0 at Gallowgate.

However, Keegan's first season wasn't all plain sailing, as he was forced to back his under-fire manager Arthur Cox after a mid-season dip in form. Two defeats in the last ten games put the Magpies on the edge of the promotion race, but in pre-play-off days that wasn't quite enough.

The eve-of-season departure of Imre Varadi was quickly forgotten as Peter Beardsley arrived, and along with Keegan and Chris Waddle went on to score a combined total of 65 league goals in the 1983/84 promotion campaign.

A memorable farewell at home to Brighton and Hove Albion when the trio all netted was followed by a friendly with Liverpool, after which a helicopter landed on the centre circle to spirit Keegan away into retirement.

Slightly less than eight years later he returned however, to rescue a club who had lost the impetus provided by promotion and were again languishing in Division Two.

Once more the uplifting effect was instant, as Keegan brought the same spirit of infectious enthusiasm he had shown as a player to his first stab at a management. Newcastle fans responded in their droves, with a doubling of the previous home attendance to 30,000 for his first game in charge – a 3–0 win over Bristol City.

However, it's sometimes forgotten that the rest of that season was a struggle, with the threat of relegation very real until the final week.

Off-field tensions also saw further intrigue – most notably a Keegan walk-out as his team were playing Swindon Town amid accusations of broken promises by Newcastle's new owners, the Hall family.

That was all forgotten the following season, however, as the team set off at a cracking pace – winning their first eleven league games before succumbing at home to Grimsby Town. Having secured promotion and taken the title, Keegan's side then gave notice of their intention to gatecrash the Premier League with a 7–1 disman-tling of Leicester City featuring hat-tricks from Andy Cole and David Kelly.

Keegan dispensed with Kelly though, re-signing Peter Beardsley to spur Cole on to a record-breaking seasonal tally of 41 goals. Cole's goals helped Newcastle to a third-place finish in the Premiership and earned the team the nickname of 'The Entertainers' (coined by Sky after a victory at Oldham Athletic in November 1993).

Sixth and second place finishes in the following two seasons kept the crowds entertained, but a visibly-aged Keegan resigned in January 1997. Various reasons were given for his shock departure, but the demands and restrictions of working for a plc remain the most plausible.

After leaving Newcastle, Keegan had spells in charge of Fulham, England and Manchester City, who he left in 2005. For three years he maintained a low profile until making a sensational return to St. James' Park in January 2008, following the sacking of Sam Allardyce.

Keegan's mere presence at an FA Cup replay with Stoke seemed to galvanize an underperforming team, as the Magpies romped to an emphatic 4–1 victory. It was a different story in the Premiership, though, as Keegan initially seemed helpless to stop an alarming slide down the table, with no win in his first seven games in charge raising the threat of relegation. However an improvement in form and a seven game unbeaten run allayed those fears and the following season began with a morale-boosting 1–1 draw against Manchester United.

Sadly, though, that proved to be another false dawn and less than a month later KK was exiting St James' Park, leaving Tyneside in turmoil. Keegan claimed that club interference had rendered his position untenable and he would later win damages for constructive dismissal at a tribunal.

Keegan has since limited his involvement in football to punditry duties with broadcaster ESPN.

Kevin Keegan factfile
Born: Armthorpe, February 14th 1951
Newcastle career: 85 apps, 49 goals (1982–84)
Other clubs: Scunthorpe United, Liverpool, Hamburg, Southampton
International: England, 63 caps, 21 goals

— SENIOR SERVICE —

First contested in 1884 when the Tyne club became the first holders by beating Rangers 4–1, the Northumberland FA Challenge Cup (later referred to as the Northumberland Senior Cup) remains an annual fixture in the North East football calendar.

Victory in the 119th staging of the Final in 2012 brought Newcastle United Reserves a record 33rd success in the competition, on their 39th appearance. Those figures would undoubtedly have been greater, however, were it not for the suspension of the competition for the duration of both World conflicts.

More significantly, the Magpies declined to enter the competition for almost half a century between 1935 and 1983, their withdrawal coming after resigning from the North Eastern League in 1933 to join the Central League.

The Northumberland FA reported at the time for a breach of rules, and both parties attended a Commission of Inquiry in London during October 1935. A settlement was reached whereby United were excused from taking part but had to pay the NFA compensation.

Resuming their Senior Cup participation in the 1984/85 season (after initial opposition from some other competing clubs), United won through to the Final in 1988, only to lose 0–1 at St James' Park. Their conquerors were Newcastle Blue Star, but their prize was a "stand-in" trophy, after the original was stolen from the Northumberland FA offices. It was later recovered.

Although most often staged at St James' Park, since United's return in 1984, they have participated in Finals at a number of local stadia including Croft Park, the Wheatsheaf Ground and Hillheads.

Final victories:
1885 Sleekburn Wanderers won 1–0 (as East End)
1889 Elswick Rangers won 3–2 (as East End) (replay after 0–0 draw, 1–2 void)
1898 Prudhoe won 5–0
1899 Burradon won 2–1
1901 Seghill won 7–0
1904 Willington Athletic won 2–0
1905 Wallsend Park Villa won 2–1
1907 Wallsend Park Villa won 4–1
1909 Newburn won 1–0 (replay after 0–0 draw)
1910 Mickley won 5–1
1911 Willington Athletic won 6–0
1912 North Shields drew 0–0 (Cup shared after two replays: 0–0 and 1–1)
1922 Preston Colliery won 8–0
1924 Blyth Spartans won 1–0
1925 Mickley won 2–1
1926 Preston Colliery won 4–2
1927 Blyth Spartans won 10–0
1929 Wallsend won 2–0
1930 Wallsend won 3–1
1931 Blyth Spartans won 1–0
1989 North Shields won 5–1
1990 North Shields won 3–0
1995 Blyth Spartans won 6–2
1996 Blyth Spartans won 3–0
1999 Blyth Spartans won 2–1
2000 Newcastle Blue Star won 4–1
2001 Bedlington Terriers won 3–1
2003 Whitley Bay won 2–0

2006 Blyth Spartans won 2–1
2008 Blyth Spartans drew 1–1 (won 4–3 on penalties)
2009 Ashington won 4–0
2011 Blyth Spartans won 4–0
2012 Team Northumbria drew 4–4 (won 4–2 on penalties)

Final defeats:
1906 North Shields Athletic lost 1–2 (replay after 1–1 draw)
1921 Ashington lost 0–2
1928 Bedlington United lost 1–2 (replay after 1–1 draw)
1935 Blyth Spartans lost 1–2 (replay after 1–1 draw)
1988 Newcastle Blue Star lost 0–1
1993 Newcastle Blue Star lost 1–2

— EXPERIENCE REQUIRED —

The following players who managed Newcastle at some stage in their career but didn't play for the club participated in the World Cup finals:

Year	Host	Player	Nation
1954	Switzerland	Bill McGarry	England
1958	Sweden	Bobby Robson	England
1962	Chile	Bobby Robson	England (non-playing)
1966	England	Jack Charlton	England
1970	Mexico	Jack Charlton	England
1974	West Germany	Kenny Dalglish	Scotland
1978	Argentina	Osvaldo Ardiles	Argentina
1978	Argentina	Graeme Souness	Scotland
1978	Argentina	Kenny Dalglish	Scotland
1982	Spain	Kenny Dalglish	Scotland
1982	Spain	Osvaldo Ardiles	Argentina
1982	Spain	Graeme Souness	Scotland
1986	Mexico	Graeme Souness	Scotland
1990	Italy	Ruud Gullit	Netherlands

— WALLSEND BOYS' CLUB —

The employees and directors of Swan Hunters Shipyard originally founded Wallsend Boys' Club in 1938 to provide recreational facilities for their apprentices and other local youngsters.

Now Swans have gone but the Boys' Club remains and still plays a key role in the local community, providing a positive influence on young people's lives.

Wallsend graduates who have gone on to join Newcastle United include:

Peter Beardsley
Ian Bogie
Lee Clark
Tony Dinning
Robbie Elliott
Chris Hedworth
Anth Lormor
Neil McDonald
David Robinson
David Roche
Alan Shearer
Eric Steele
Paul Stephenson
Alan Thompson
Steve Watson
John Watson
Jeff Wrightson
Michael Bridges
Fraser Forster
Steven Taylor

Former player Alan Shearer didn't forget his roots and Wallsend were among a large number of organisations to benefit from the proceeds of his 2006 testimonial match and other events, being awarded £15,000.

A certain other United have also indirectly benefited from the Wallsend production line, with Steve Bruce and Michael Carrick finding their way to Premiership-winning success at Old Trafford. All told, over 65 former Wallsend youngsters have gone on to play league football to date.

— GONG SHOW —

Newcastle United players and managers who have been recognised with civil or military honours include:

Recipient	Award	Year/event
Sandy Higgins	Military Medal	World War I
Tom Rowlandson	Military Cross	World War I

Donald Bell	Victoria Cross	World War I
Benny Craig	Military Medal	World War II
Ivor Allchurch	MBE	1966
Jack Charlton	OBE	1974
George Eastham	OBE	1975
Kevin Keegan	OBE	1982
Kenny Dalglish	MBE	1984
Bobby Robson	CBE	1990
Peter Beardsley	MBE	1995
Ian Rush	MBE	1996
John Barnes	MBE	1998
Stuart Pearce	MBE	1999
Alan Shearer	OBE	2001
Bobby Robson	Knighthood	2002
Les Ferdinand	MBE	2005

In addition, former Newcastle United Chairman John Hall was knighted in 1991.

Sir Bobby Robson was awarded an honorary degree by Newcastle University in 2003, becoming a Doctor of Civil Law (DCL). The same accolade was then bestowed upon Alan Shearer in 2006 by Northumbria University, with city neighbours Newcastle University following suit in 2009.

Fellow former Magpies manager Jackie Charlton has amassed no less than four free degrees meanwhile: from the University of Limerick (1994), Northumbria University and Leeds Metropolitan University (both in 2003) and Leeds University (2004).

— TEENAGE KICKS PART II —

Newcastle United's second successful FA Youth Cup campaign came in the 1984/85 season, beginning with a resounding 6–0 home victory over then holders Everton. Future Magpies star Paul Gascoigne notched two in that game and scored another when Leeds United were beaten 2–0 on Tyneside in the fourth round.

The Fifth Round pitted United against Manchester City and that man Gazza was on target again as a 2–1 success was recorded. Newcastle's name came out of the hat first at the fourth time of asking, with Coventry City promptly dispatched 3–0 – two goals for Gascoigne this time round.

Into the last four and Birmingham City were beaten 2–0 at home, before a resounding 5–2 win at St Andrew's set up a final against Watford.

Just under 7,000 fans were at St James' Park to see a 0–0 stalemate, the young Hornets being captained by future Newcastle striker Malcolm Allen. There were to be no mistakes in the away leg though, with Joe Allon and Gascoigne netting two apiece in a 4–1 victory for Colin Suggett's side in front of over 7,000 fans at Vicarage Road.

Seven of the final side went on to feature in the Magpies first team: Joe Allon, Paul Gascoigne, Gary Kelly, Tony Nesbit, Kevin Scott, Brian Tinnion, Jeff Wrightson. An eighth – Paul Stephenson – was on the bench. The other three players were: Stuart Dickinson, Tony Hayton and Stephen Forster.

And a further trio of players featured in ties leading up the final, these being future first team player Ian Bogie, Peter Harbach and Ian McKenzie.

— LEADING BY EXAMPLE —

Newcastle managers have taken to the field on a number of occasions in non-competitive games to show their charges just how it's done. These include:

Charlie Mitten
The former Manchester United and Fulham player celebrated the end of his first season in charge of the Magpies in May 1959 by getting his boots on. United played a three game tour of Southern Ireland, with Mitten scoring once in a 6–3 victory over Drumcondra.

Ossie Ardiles
A midweek friendly at Blyth Spartans in November 1991 gave World Cup winner Ossie the chance to pull his boots on. Ardiles was joined in the Newcastle side by his assistant manager Tony Galvin (ex-Tottenham Hotspur) and also kit man Chris Guthrie (ex-Fulham). And Ossie repeated his performance in January 1992, forming a three-man defence with Galvin and Magpies coach Derek Fazackerley as United took part in a game staged to inaugurate the new floodlights at local league Dunston Federation Brewery.

Kevin Keegan
Putting aside the disappointment of losing the Premiership title just days before, KK pulled on a black and white shirt at the City Ground

to take part in Stuart Pearce's testimonial. The final score on an enjoyable evening was 6–5 to Pearce's Forest, with Keegan netting from the penalty spot for the black and whites.

Kevin Keegan and Kenny Dalglish

With Ruud Gullit crying off due to an unspecified illness, his two managerial predecessors both made cameo appearances for Newcastle during Peter Beardsley's testimonial game at St James' Park. For Kenny it was a chance to face his former side Celtic, although both men would have appreciated the original choice of opposition – Liverpool (who were forced to pull out due to league fixture congestion).

Ruud Gullit

Having seen his side beaten in their two previous warm-up games at Dundee United and Livingston, Ruud Gullit's patience ran out when his side trailed 0–2 at half-time away to Reading in July 1999. Withdrawing defender David Beharall from the action, Gullit emerged for the second half to try and organise his failing troops from midfield. A penalty conversion just after the hour from James Coppinger halved the arrears and a late solo effort from Paul Robinson saved the Magpies' blushes, the game ending 2–2.

Gullit then repeated the trick four nights later away at Stoke City, wearing shirt number 16 and replacing Des Hamilton after 38 minutes. He remained on the field for the rest of the evening, although in the final 30 minutes he moved further forward. One attempt at a shot saw the ball fly high and wide of the goal into an unoccupied part of the Britannia Stadium – the game being held up until a replacement ball was found.

— NO PLACE LIKE HOME —

With more and more domestic fixtures taking place in identikit stadia, here is a list of now-defunct grounds that have featured on the club's seasonal itinerary at one time or another since league football resumed in 1946. Many of them have now been replaced by housing estates, supermarkets or just levelled and left – but memories of them remain.

Opponent	Venue	Last visited
Arsenal	Highbury	2005
Bolton Wanderers	Burnden Park	1995

Bradford Park Avenue	Park Avenue	1947
Brighton and Hove Albion	Goldstone Ground	1991
Bristol Rovers	Eastville	1980
Cardiff City	Ninian Park	1983
Chester City	Sealand Road	1974
Chesterfield	Saltergate	1947
Colchester United	Layer Road	1982
Coventry City	Highfield Road	2000
Derby County	The Baseball Ground	1996
Doncaster Rovers	Belle Vue	1947
Huddersfield Town	Leeds Road	1984
Hull City	Boothferry Park	1990
Leicester City	Filbert Street	2002
Manchester City	Maine Road	2002
Middlesbrough	Ayresome Park	1992
Millwall	The Den	1993
Newport County	Somerton Park	1947
Northampton Town	The County Ground	1966
Oxford United	The Manor Ground	1992
Reading	Elm Park	1990
Rotherham United	Millmoor	1993
Scunthorpe United	The Old Showground	1974
Shrewsbury Town	Gay Meadow	1984
Southampton	The Dell	2000
Stoke City	The Victoria Ground	1995
Sunderland	Roker Park	1996
Swansea City	Vetch Field	1983
Walsall	Fellows Park	1975
Wigan Athletic	Springfield Park	1954
Wimbledon	Plough Lane	1989

Note: Dates given are of the last competitive first team game Newcastle played at the venue. The Magpies have appeared in friendlies at other grounds which no longer exist but never played competitively there – hence their omission from the list.

— LIGHT YEARS —

Initially installed in 1951 for training sessions only, simple spot lamps mounted on telegraph poles were first used to illuminate a game at St James' Park when Celtic provided the opposition in a friendly match in

1953. Eighty 1,000 watt lights were installed by local contractors Fletcher Brothers to illuminate the playing surface, whilst extra wiring had to be installed at the turnstiles and in the West Stand. And at half-time they were switched off, with the only light visible the thousands of tiny orange glows as many of the 41,888 present puffed away on their cigarettes!

United's programme editor noted at the time that "floodlit football may have a great future" and was later moved to write that, "floodlighting has certainly revealed unexpected beauty of form and colour as well as motion in football".

The staging of a first-round replay between Carlisle and Darlington in November 1955 saw St James' become the first venue to host an FA Cup tie between league sides under floodlights, and after the Football League sanctioned their use United played in the first competitive league game under lights, against Portsmouth at Fratton Park in February 1956.

March 1958 saw a new system installed at St James' Park, consisting of floodlighting attached to four towers erected on each corner of the stadium, at a total cost of £40,000. At the time the highest in the UK at over 190ft, these were visible across the city and became a familiar part of the landscape. All four towers were located on the terraces, alterations to the Leazes End roof allowing the pair at the end to poke through.

Following the opening of the new East Stand in 1973, extra lighting on its roof came into use, allowing the removal of the north-east tower when the old Leazes End was flattened in 1978. Meanwhile, the north-west tower was relocated outside the ground on the adjacent car park and the south-east pylon was also dismantled, leaving SJP with two towers in the 1980s.

Two then became one in the summer of 1987, when the north-west tower was dismantled ahead of demolition work on the west side of the stadium. And the completion of the Milburn Stand and commissioning of roof-mounted lighting saw the south-west tower felled, after almost 30 years' service.

— MEN OF LETTERS —

Some of the more elongated formal names of Newcastle players have included:

Full name	AKA
Faustino Hernan Hinestroza **Asprilla**	Tino
Carlos Daniel Lobo **Cordone**	Daniel

Diego Antonio **Gavilan** Zarate	Diego
Fransiscus Leonardus Albertus **Koenen**	Frans
Elena Sierra **Marcelino**	Martha
Obafemi Akinwunmi **Martins**	Oba
Francisco Ernandi Lima da Silva **Mirandinha**	Mira
Francisco Jiménez Tejada	Xisco
Nolberto Albino **Solano** Todco	Nobby
Hugo Miguel Ferreira **Viana**	Hugo

In January 1997, United announced that the Portuguese central defender Raul Oliveira had passed a medical and was set to sign on loan from Farense. However, the deal fell through and Oliveira later appeared briefly for Bradford City, before returning to Portugal. The player's full name was: Raul Miguel Silva da Fonseca Castanheira de Oliveira.

At the opposite end of the scale, the club took goalkeeper An Qi on trial in December 2002 from Chinese club Dalian Shide, but didn't offer him a contract.

— THERE'S ONLY TWO —

Brothers who have played for Newcastle United over the years include:

Ameobi   The introduction of Sammy Ameobi as a substitute during Newcastle's 2–2 draw at Stamford Bridge in May 2011 saw him appear alongside elder brother Shola – the first time in 58 years that siblings had played together in a league game for the club. There was a third, middle, Ameobi brother on United's books, but Tomi failed to make it through to the first team and was released in 2005.

Appleby   Teessiders Matty and Richie were at St James' Park together in the early 1990s, but while the elder Matty appeared for the first team in defence, the younger Richie never got the chance to show his midfield skills in a competitive senior game. However, the duo were selected in the same team by Kevin Keegan in Anglo-Italian Cup ties away to Bari and at home to Cesena in 1992.

Caldwell   Despite playing together at junior and reserve level, the nearest central defenders Steve and Gary got to partnering each other in the first team came when Sir Bobby Robson brought them both off the bench during a testimonial match at West Bromwich Albion in 2001. After the pair had left United, they appeared together competitively for the first time at senior level when both were selected for Scotland in a World Cup qualifier away to Moldova in October 2004.

King   Amble-born goalkeeper Ray and his elder striker brother George were both at Gallowgate when World War II ended but never played in the first team together.

Robledo   Chilean pair George and Eduardo ('Ted') were signed from Barnsley in January 1949, United taking the younger left-sided midfielder Ted in order to capture the signature of his striker brother. The brothers appeared together for the first time in a Newcastle shirt on the last day of 1949, away to Aston Villa.

Withe   Merseyside-born duo Peter and Chris were on the books at St James' Park together in the 1970s, but the younger Chris (a defender) only made his first team debut the season after the older Peter (a striker) had left.

The following sets of brothers were on the club's books together, but only the Kennedy brothers both appeared in the football league.

Elliott	Robbie and John
Hislop	Shaka and Kona
Howie	Jimmy and David
Keating	Bert and Reg
Kennedy	Alan and Keith
Lindsay	Billy and James
Mitten	John and Charles junior
Rutherford	Jackie and Andrew
Smith	'Tot', George and Robert
Wilson	Joe and Glenn

— NEWCASTLE LEGENDS: STAN SEYMOUR —

TOON LEGENDS

STAN SEYMOUR

Stan Seymour: Gave his life to Newcastle United

As captain, manager, director and Vice-President, Seymour served Newcastle United in three spells over a period of almost 70 years.

The man known as 'Mister Newcastle' thanks to his achievements on and off the field was initially discarded by the Magpies as a teenage amateur player before World War I, returning to play local football for Shildon.

After a brief spell at Bradford City, Seymour's career took off after some impressive displays for Greenock Morton, before a move to Newcastle followed in May 1920.

The return on the £2,500 fee was instant as Seymour marked his debut with a goal on the opening day of the season, although his side only managed a 1–1 home draw with West Bromwich Albion.

Four solid seasons in the Newcastle side at outside-left brought successive top ten finishes, culminating in a 2–0 victory in the 1924 FA Cup Final, where Seymour scored the second goal in the dying minutes of the club's Wembley debut.

Seymour's finest campaign, however, came in 1926/27 when he was an ever-present in Newcastle's championship-winning side, scoring 18 goals in the process – the last of which gave his team the 1–1 draw that clinched the title away to West Ham United.

He retired from playing two seasons later, his final appearance coming at Gallowgate against Arsenal in October 1928.

In 1937 Seymour was invited to join the Newcastle board of directors. He accepted, giving up his sideline of reporting on matches for newspapers but retaining ownership of the sports shop he'd established in the city.

After the war years intervened, Seymour set about reconstructing the side which achieved promotion back to the First Division at the second attempt in 1948.

Having handed over nominal control of team affairs to George Martin, Seymour took over again when Martin defected to Aston Villa in 1950, presiding over two Wembley FA Cup Final successes.

A dip in results, however, led to Seymour being persuaded by his fellow directors to try another team manager, Duggie Livingstone arriving in December 1954.

He was to last barely a year though, with Seymour famously over-ruling him before the 1955 FA Cup Final, when the name of Jackie Milburn failed to appear on the first Newcastle teamsheet submitted to the directors.

Seymour remained at St James' Park while Charlie Mitten and Norman Smith were tried in the manager's job. However, his master-stroke proved to be bringing Joe Harvey back to Tyneside in 1962 – the former Magpies captain having been overlooked for the post when Mitten was appointed, moving on to learn his trade at Workington.

With Harvey's departure in 1975, Seymour retired as a director the following year at the age of 83. He passed away two years later, having seen his son join the board – although he didn't live to see Stan Seymour junior emulate his father and become chairman.

George Stanley Seymour factfile
Born: Kelloe, County Durham, May 16th 1893
Died: December 24th 1978
Newcastle career: 1920–29
Other clubs: Shildon Town, Coxhoe, Bradford City, Greenock Morton

— TREBLES ALL ROUND – FA CUP —

Eighteen players have scored FA Cup hat-tricks for the Magpies since their first entry into the competition under that name in January 1893 (a 2–3 home defeat at the hands of Middlesbrough). The full list is as follows:

Player	Season	Opponent
Bill Appleyard	1907/08	Grimsby Town (h)
George Wilson	1908/09	Clapton Orient (h)
Albert Shepherd	1910/11	Bury (h)
Neil Harris	1923/24	Derby County (h)
Hughie Gallacher	1926/27	Notts County (h)
Tom McDonald	1926/27	Notts County (h)
Jimmy Richardson	1929/30	Clapton Orient (h)
Hughie Gallacher	1929/30	Brighton & Hove Albion (h)
Duncan Hutchison	1930/31	Nottingham Forest (h)
Jimmy Richardson	1931/32	Southport (n)
Charlie Wayman	1946/47	Southampton (h)
Jackie Milburn	1949/50	Oldham Athletic (a)
Jackie Milburn	1951/52	Portsmouth (a)
Len White	1957/58	Plymouth Argyle (a)
Duncan Neale	1960/61	Fulham (h)
Wyn Davies	1966/67	Coventry City (a)
Paul Kitson	1994/95	Swansea City (h)
Peter Lovenkrands	2009/10	Plymouth Argyle (h)

In addition, Andy Aitken netted four times in an FA Cup qualifying round home tie against local side Willington Athletic in season 1897/98. By the end of the 2011/12 season, the club had played 365 matches in the FA Cup. 178 victories, 85 draws and 102 losses have been recorded, with 659 goals scored and 446 conceded.

— TREBLES ALL ROUND – LEAGUE CUP —

Player	Season	Opponent	Goals scored
Alan Gowling	1975/76	Southport (h)	4
Malcolm Macdonald	1973/74	Doncaster Rovers (h)	3
Malcolm Macdonald	1974/75	Queens Park Rangers (h)	3
Gavin Peacock	1991/92	Crewe Alexandra (a)	3
Andy Cole	1993/94	Notts County (h)	3
Andy Cole	1993/94	Notts County (a)	3
Craig Bellamy	2001/02	Brentford (h)	3

— TWIN TOWERS PART III —

As well as their various cup final and semi-final outings, a Newcastle side has also appeared at Wembley on another occasion, as part of The Football League Centenary celebrations of 1988.

The Mercantile Credit Football Festival was a two-day knock-out event involving 16 teams, who played each other in limited duration (20 minutes each way) games on a reduced size pitch.

Qualification for the event was based on the number of league points gained during a three month period earlier in the season from Divisions One to Four – eight clubs joining from the First, four from the Second and two each from Divisions Three and Four.

The event took place over a Saturday and Sunday when no league games were scheduled. And in what was already the second game of the day, Newcastle kicked off at 10.50am before a sparsely populated Wembley against Liverpool.

Newcastle's squad included: Gary Kelly, John Anderson, Brian Tinnion, John Bailey, Glenn Roeder, Paul Gascoigne, Paul Goddard, Mirandinha, Michael O'Neill, Neil McDonald, Paul Stephenson and John Cornwell. After a 0–0 draw the tie was settled on penalties – but in a change to the usual practice, these were sudden death from the off.

Steve McMahon took the first Liverpool spot-kick, only for Kelly's outstretched boot to deny him. Neil McDonald then stepped up to beat future Newcastle custodian Mike Hooper and United had a rare – if bizarre – success under the Twin Towers to celebrate.

In the second game later the same day though, the black and whites came back down to earth with a bump though, losing to Fourth Division Tranmere Rovers. The side from Birkenhead netted through John Morrissey and an Ian Muir penalty and Toon misery was complete when Eric Nixon denied McDonald from the spot.

Tranmere were so up for it that they'd even recorded a tune for their Wembley bow (*We are the Rovers* by Don Woods) and had beaten Division One side Wimbledon in their first game. With many of the 1,000 or so Newcastle followers there having purchased weekend tickets, the Sunday saw them trudge back again for a further day of pointless games not involving their own club.

Nottingham Forest were the eventual winners of the competition, but their manager Brian Clough was so uninterested in proceedings that he declined to attend.

— DREAM STARTS II —

Two Newcastle players have made their senior debuts as substitutes and scored as follows:

Alex Mathie made his way off the bench at St James' Park in September 1993 with his side trailing 1–2 to Sheffield Wednesday during the club's maiden season of Premier League involvement. Arriving on 62 minutes, he had a hand in his side's equaliser before conjuring a glorious 81st-minute volley at the Leazes End to put Newcastle 3–2 up. Clad in their blue change kit, United ran out 4–2 winners.

Papiss Demba Cisse was introduced as a 14th-minute replacement against Aston Villa in a Premier League encounter at St James' Park in February 2012. The Senegal international forward then netted the winning goal in a 2–1 success on 71 minutes, thumping a sublime left-footed drive into the top corner of the Gallowgate goal. As was the case in 1993, the game was live on Sky TV.

George Dalton netted within six minutes of his debut, at home to Leicester City in 1961. Unfortunately it was an own goal.

Aside from the select few players who scored at least a hat trick on their first competitive appearance for Newcastle, a number of others have also marked their debut in memorable style by bagging two goals:

Year	Player	Opponent/venue
1906	Finlay Speedie	The Wednesday (h)
1907	George Wilson	Liverpool (a)
1925	Hughie Gallacher	Everton (h)
1946	George Stobbart	Coventry City (h)
1946	Jackie Milburn	Barnsley (h)
1958	Arthur Bottom	Everton (a)

1958	Ivor Allchurch	Leicester City (h)
1960	Duncan Neale	Fulham (h)
1998	Duncan Ferguson	Wimbledon (h)

— SHARP SHOOTERS —

Newcastle's top goalscorers for each season of Premier League participation are as follows (cup goals not included in totals):

1993/1994	Andy Cole (34)
1994/1995	Peter Beardsley (12)
1995/1996	Les Ferdinand (25)
1996/1997	Alan Shearer (25)
1997/1998	John Barnes (6)
1998/1999	Alan Shearer (14)
1999/2000	Alan Shearer 23)
2000/2001	Carl Cort & Nolberto Solano (both 6)
2001/2002	Alan Shearer (23)
2002/2003	Alan Shearer (17)
2003/2004	Alan Shearer (22)
2004/2005	Alan Shearer & Craig Bellamy (both 7)
2005/2006	Alan Shearer (10)
2006/2007	Obafemi Martins (11)
2007/2008	Michael Owen (11)
2008/2009	Obafemi Martins & Michael Owen (both 8)
2010/2011	Kevin Nolan (12)
2011/2012	Demba Ba (16)

— IT'S A FAMILY AFFAIR II —

The following families have had fathers and sons who have represented
Newcastle:

Edgar   Goalkeeper Eddie made one first team appearance in
1976 before emigrating to Canada. His son David (a
defender) was born in Kitchener, Ontario but moved
to Newcastle and came through the ranks to make his
first team debut in December 2006.

Wilson   Defender Joseph and his centre forward son Carl both
made a single league appearance for Newcastle's first

team – the latter the only one of seven footballing brothers to emulate his father.

Other fathers and sons who have both been on the club's books, include:

Cahill	Tommy and Tommy Junior
Gallacher	Hughie, Hughie junior and Matt
McDermott	Terry, Neale and Greg
McDonald*	James and Neil
Nattrass	Irving and Paul
Niblo	Tom and Alan
Seymour	Stan and Colin
Swinburne	Tom, Alan and Trevor
Wharton	Kenny and Paul
Wrightson	Jeff and Kieran

Note: Second (and third) named didn't play first team football for the club except*, where the father failed but the son succeeded.

— MANX MAGS —

Back in the 1980s when competitive fixtures for Newcastle got no more exotic than trips to Wales, friendly tours provided some variety and a change of scenery for the more intrepid supporter. However, the loyalty of the most diehard Magpie follower was tested when the club opted to participate in the Isle of Man Tournament as part of their pre-season programme in both 1985 and 1986.

Newcastle's first appearance in the tournament coincided with a summer season on the island from singer Tony Christie, while the following year featured cabaret delights in the shape of Les Dennis, Max Boyce and Rod Hull and Emu!

1985:

Venue	Fixture/result	Newcastle scorer(s)
Douglas	Leicester City 3 Newcastle 2	Peter Beardsley, George Reilly
Ramsey	Blackburn Rovers 2 Newcastle 1	Paul Gascoigne
Castletown	Wigan Athletic 1 Newcastle 4	Neil McDonald 2, Glenn Roeder, Peter Beardsley

1986:

Venue	Fixture/result	Newcastle scorer(s)
Douglas	Blackburn Rovers 2	Paul Gascoigne,
	Newcastle 2	Neil McDonald
Castletown	Portsmouth 2	Neil McDonald,
	Newcastle 2	Joe Allon
Castletown	Isle of Man XI 1	Ian Stewart,
	Newcastle 5	Peter Beardsley
		Joe Allon 2, Paul Ferris

— BIG DAY OUT IN THE NORTH —

A selection of crucial final fixtures at St James' Park over the years – crucial for the opposition that is:

April 1903 Requiring a victory on Tyneside to retain the First Division title, Sunderland blew their big chance by losing 1–0 to Newcastle. The Wearsiders' defeat meant they finished third behind title winners The Wednesday and runners-up Aston Villa.

May 1926 Having lost the FA Cup final on the previous Saturday, Manchester City arrived at Gallowgate needing to avoid defeat in order to secure their First Division status. Sadly for them, the game finished in a 3–2 victory for Newcastle with City missing a penalty.

April 1949 A resounding 5–0 away success by Portsmouth confirmed the status of the south coast team as Division One champions, Jack Froggatt leading the way with a hat-trick.

April 1962 The start of the Don Revie era of success came at St James' Park as Leeds United won 3–0 to banish any fear of relegation to Division Three (although other results meant they were safe regardless of the score). The visitors led at the interval thanks to an own goal, with second half efforts from Billy McAdams and Albert Johanneson securing victory. Just three years later Leeds were runners-up in Division One.

May 1968 Manchester City were pressed all the way by the home side before triumphing 4–3 to lift the First Division title, thanks to goals from Neil Young (2), Mike Summerbee and Francis Lee.

May 1979 The penultimate home game of the season saw the gate increase by some 19,000 to over 28,000 as Malcolm Allison brought his Brighton and Hove Albion side to Tyneside. Having been at St James' Park the previous Wednesday to watch Newcastle beat Bristol

Rovers 3–0, The Seagulls raced into a similar lead before the interval after Brian Horton, Peter Ward and Gerry Ryan all netted.

And although Alan Shoulder reduced the arrears after the break, Brighton were never in danger of losing the points that confirmed their promotion to Division One for the first time in their history, behind title winners Crystal Palace.

— WE ONLY HAD TEN MEN —

Prior to the end of the 2011/12 season, 57 players had been dismissed while appearing for Newcastle United in their 692 Premiership fixtures. Five of those decisions were subsequently rescinded. The full list is:

Year	Player	Fixture/venue	Result
1993	Pavel Srnicek	Coventry City (a)	lost 1–2
1994	Pavel Srnicek	Leicester City (a)	won 3–1
1994	Philippe Albert	Liverpool (h)	drew 1–1
1995	Robert Lee	Everton (a)	lost 0–2
1995	Pavel Srnicek	Tottenham Hotspur (h)	drew 3–3
1995	John Beresford	Everton (h)	won 1–0
1996	David Batty	Chelsea (a)	drew 1–1
1997	Keith Gillespie	Arsenal (a)	won 1–0
1997	David Batty	Aston Villa (h)	won 1–0
1997	David Batty	Derby County (a)	lost 0–1
1998	David Batty	Blackburn Rovers (a)	lost 0–1
1998	Nicos Dabizas	Arsenal (a)	lost 0–3
1998	Stuart Pearce	West Ham United (h)	lost 0–3
1998	Didi Hamann	Liverpool (a)	lost 2–4
1999	Nicos Dabizas	Charlton Athletic (a)	drew 2–2
1999	Alan Shearer	Aston Villa (h)	lost 0–1
1999	Nicos Dabizas	Manchester United (a)	lost 1–5
1999	Warren Barton	Coventry City (a)	lost 1–4
2000	Warren Barton	Derby County (h)	won 3–2
2001	Nolberto Solano	Tottenham Hotspur (a)	lost 2–4
2001	Kieron Dyer	Tottenham Hotspur (a)	lost 2–4
2001	Nolberto Solano	Ipswich Town (a)	lost 0–1
2001	Gary Speed*	Aston Villa (h)	won 3–0
2001	Alan Shearer*	Charlton Athletic (a)	drew 1–1
2001	Craig Bellamy*	Arsenal (a)	won 3–1
2002	Nicos Dabizas	Blackburn Rovers (a)	lost 2–5

2003	Laurent Robert	Arsenal (h)	drew 1–1
2003	Andy Griffin	Fulham (a)	lost 1–2
2003	Laurent Robert	Everton (a)	drew 2–2
2003	Andy O'Brien	Chelsea (a)	lost 0–5
2004	Andy O'Brien	Aston Villa (a)	drew 0–0
2004	Lee Bowyer	Liverpool (a)	lost 1–3
2005	Lee Bowyer	Aston Villa (h)	lost 0–3
2005	Kieron Dyer	Aston Villa (h)	lost 0–3
2005	Steven Taylor	Aston Villa (h)	lost 0–3
2005	Shola Ameobi	Everton (a)	lost 0–2
2005	Jermaine Jenas*	Arsenal (a)	lost 0–2
2005	Scott Parker	Fulham (a)	drew 1–1
2005	Steven Taylor	Blackburn Rovers (a)	won 3–0
2005	Lee Bowyer	Liverpool (a)	lost 0–2
2006	Celestine Babayaro	Aston Villa (a)	won 2–1
2006	Jean-Alain Boumsong	Liverpool (h)	lost 1–3
2006	Stephen Carr	Chelsea (h)	won 1–0
2006	Titus Bramble	Everton (h)	drew 1–1
2008	Alan Smith	Manchester United (a)	lost 0–6
2008	Danny Guthrie	Hull City (h)	Lost 1–2
2008	Habib Beye*	Manchester City (h)	Drew 2–2
2008	Sebastien Bassong	Wigan Athletic (a)	Lost 1–2
2009	Nicky Butt	Blackburn Rovers (a)	Lost 0–3
2009	Kevin Nolan	Everton (h)	Drew 0–0
2009	Joey Barton	Liverpool (a)	Lost 0–3
2009	Sebastien Bassong	Fulham (h)	Lost 0–1
2009	David Edgar	Aston Villa (a)	Lost 0–1
2010	Fabricio Coloccini	Bolton Wanderers (a)	Lost 1–5
2011	Ryan Taylor	Bolton Wanderers (h)	Drew 1–1
2011	Jonas Gutierrez	Manchester United (a)	Drew 1–1
2011	Dan Gosling	Norwich City (a)	Lost 2–4

*Subsequently rescinded

Saturday April 2nd 2005 remains Newcastle's blackest day in the Premiership, with Bowyer and Dyer dismissed for fighting with each other in the 82nd minute of the game. That reduced the Magpies to eight men, Steven Taylor having been red carded nine minutes previously by referee Barry Knight for deliberate handball.

In addition, there has been one instance of a Newcastle player being red carded while not on the field of play. This came in October 2005 at St James' Park when a case of mistaken identity saw Scott Parker wrongly yellow carded. When the error was realised post-match, the booking was transferred to the guilty party, Stephen Carr, who had already been booked in the game and was subsequently banned.

— SINGLETOONS —

The following 60 players made one league start for Newcastle United but never featured in any other competitive game for the club.

Name	Year	Name	Year
J W Barr	1893	M. Keir	1893
John Patten	1893	Alex Ramsay	1893
Isaac Ryder	1893	William Simm	1893
Haynes	1895	Thomas Blyth	1897
John Allen	1898	Archie Mowatt	1898
George Mole	1900	Daniel Pattinson	1902
Ord Richardson	1902	Bob Benson	1903
Hugh Bolton	1905	Tom Rowlandson	1905
R.E. Rutherford	1906	George Hedley	1907
Ben Nicholson	1907	Noel Brown	1908
Bob Blanthorne	1908	William Hughes	1908
Alex McCulloch	1908	Jack Thomas	1912
Jack Alderson	1913	Thomas Grey	1914
Tom Cairns	1915	John Soulsby	1915
Alex Rainnie	1920	John Thain	1921
John Archibald	1922	Allan Taylor	1925
Billy Halliday	1927	Stan Barber	1928
Robert Bradley	1928	Joe Wilson	1929
Ike Keen	1930	James Robinson	1931
Joe Ford	1932	Tom McBain	1932
David Smith	1936	John Shiel	1937
George Bradley	1938	Dominic Kelly	1939
Ron Anderson	1947	Albert Clark	1948
Andy Graver	1950	Alex Gaskell	1953
Bill Redhead	1956	Chris Harker	1958
Carl Wilson	1958	Grant Malcolm	1959
George Watkin	1962	Les O'Neil	1963
John Hope	1969	Keith Kennedy	1972

Tony Bell	1974	Rob McKinnon	1985*
Paul Moran	1991*		

*substituted during the game

In addition, five players made their only Newcastle appearance as substitutes in league games:

Martin Gorry	1977
Keith Mulgrove	1978
Kevin Pugh	1981
John Watson	1991
James Coppinger	2000

Another six players made their only appearance for the club in the League Cup:

Billy Wilson	1961
Derek Craig	1971
Phil Leaver	1980
Justin Fashanu	1991 (as sub)
Steve Guppy	1994 (as sub)
Rob Elliot	2011

One more player made his sole outing to date in the UEFA Cup:

Lewis Guy	2004 (as sub)

And finally, the FA Cup saw two debutants who never appeared again:

Eddie Edgar	1976
Phil Airey	2011 (as sub)

Perhaps the most luckless trio of 'singletoons' are Thomas Blyth, George Mole and Daniel Pattinson – who all marked their only game for the club by scoring a goal.

James Coppinger's Premiership experience consisted of 11 minutes at home to Chelsea, while fellow striker Lewis Guy played for exactly the same duration at home to Sporting Lisbon in the UEFA Cup. The pair subsequently played together when both moved on to Doncaster Rovers.

— CLOSE BUT . . . —

Players who were selected as first team substitutes for Newcastle United but failed to make a competitive senior appearance include:

Player	Season(s) selected
Terry Melling	1965/66
Terry Johnson	1968/69
Dave Clarke	1968/69
Billy Coulson	1971/72
Brian Reid	1993/94
Jason Drysdale	1994/95
Paul Barrett	1996/97
Stuart Elliott	1996/97, 1997/98
David Terrier	1997/98
Ralf Keidel	1997/98
Brian Pinas	1997/98
Lionel Perez	1998/99, 1999/00
Peter Keen	1998/99
Gary Caldwell	1999/00, 2000/01
Stuart Green	1999/00, 2001/02
Tony Caig	2002/03, 2003/04, 2004/05
Bradley Orr	2003/04
Kris Gate	2005/06
James Troisi	2006/07, 2007/08
Fraser Forster	2006/07
Frank Wiafe Danquah	2008/09
Mark Doninger	2008/09
Brad Inman	2008/09, 2009/10
Wesley Ngo Baheng	2009/10
Ole Soderberg	2009/10, 2010/11, 2011/12
Michael Richardson	2010/11
Paul Dummett	2011/12
Jeff Henderson	2011/12

— ONLY THE LOANEES —

Players who have moved from other clubs for temporary stints in a Newcastle shirt include:

Player	Loaned from	Year
Viv Busby	Luton Town	1971
Alex Cropley	Aston Villa	1980
Alan Brown	Sunderland	1981
David Mills	West Bromwich Albion	1982

Howard Gayle	Liverpool	1982
Martin Thomas	Bristol Rovers	1983
Ian Baird	Southampton	1984
Dave McKellar	Hibernian	1986
Darren Bradshaw	York City	1989
Tommy Gaynor	Nottingham Forest	1990
Dave Mitchell	Chelsea	1991
Paul Moran	Tottenham Hotspur	1991
Andy Walker	Celtic	1991
Gavin Maguire	Portsmouth	1991
Paul Bodin	Crystal Palace	1991
Terry Wilson	Nottingham Forest	1992
Brian Kilcline	Oldham Athletic	1992
Brian Reid	Glasgow Rangers	1994
Tommy Wright	Manchester City	1999
Helder	Deportivo La Coruna	1999
Wayne Quinn	Sheffield United	2001
Sylvain Distin	Paris St.Germain	2001
Michael Bridges	Leeds United	2004
Giuseppe Rossi	Manchester United	2006
Oguchi Onyewu	Standard Liege	2007

Of these players, Mills, Thomas, Bradshaw, Kilcline and Quinn were ultimately signed by Newcastle on permanent contracts. Attempts were made to sign both Brown and Distin – the former returning to Wearside after allegedly failing a medical amid rumours the Magpies lacked the funds to fund the deal.

Distin, on the other hand, opted not to prolong his stay at Gallowgate despite offers to do so and a £4m transfer fee having been agreed with his club. He moved on to newly-promoted Manchester City, with Newcastle lodging a formal complaint of 'tapping up' allegations. Even since then, Distin has been the target for vocal abuse from Newcastle supporters when he has played for City against his former club.

One player who was never in danger of being offered a contract was Paul Moran, who made one ill-starred appearance at home to Wolverhampton Wanderers and was soon on his way back to White Hart Lane.

— BRIEF ENCOUNTERS II —

A further selection of some of the more exotic players who spent time on trial with Newcastle United but never appeared for the club competitively:

Player	Country of Birth
Bernard Allou	Ivory Coast
Teoman Arika	Turkey
Paulo Baier	Brazil
Jean-Hugues Ateba Bilayi	Cameroon
Jorge Bohme	Germany
Dries Boussatta	Morocco
Pierre Boya	Cameroon
Erol Bulut	Germany
Francesco Coco	Italy
Costas Costa	Cyprus
George Christouplos	Australia
Garra Dembele	Mali
John Doyle	USA
Jan Eriksson	Sweden
Carlos Sierra Fumero	Spain
Wael Gomaa	Egypt
Sergei Gurenko	Belarus
Ove Hansen	Denmark
Esteban Herrera	Argentina
Martin Hidalgo	Peru
Leo Houtsanan	Finland
Thomas Huschbeck	Germany
Sami Hyppia	Finland
Rodney Jack	Jamaica
Sun Jihai	China

— CLUB TRIPS —

Newcastle United have regularly embarked upon pre and post-season tours to an array of overseas destinations, where they've played numerous friendly matches:

Year	Destination
1904	Denmark
1905	Bohemia

1906	Bohemia
1907	Germany
1909	Denmark
1911	Germany/Switzerland
1913	Denmark
1921	Spain/France
1922	Norway/Sweden/Denmark
1924	Spain
1927	Holland
1929	Austria/Czechoslovakia/Hungary
1932	France/Germany
1946	Norway/Sweden
1949	USA/Canada
1952	Southern Africa
1955	West Germany
1956	Spain/West Germany
1958	Spain/Romania
1959	Southern Ireland
1959	Spain (Mallorca)*
1960	West Germany/Yugoslavia/Spain
1965	Denmark/West Germany
1970	USA/Canada
1972	Thailand/Hong Kong/Iran
1976	Norway
1977	Malta
1977	Holland*
1978	Sweden*
1980	Sweden*
1982	Portugal (Madeira)*
1983	Malaysia/Thailand/Japan
1983	West Germany/Greece*
1985	New Zealand/Fiji
1988	Sweden*
1989	Sweden*
1990	Hungary (Budapest)*
1991	Sweden*
1994	Finland*
1996	Thailand/Singapore/Japan*
1999	Holland*
2000	Trinidad/Tobago

2000	USA*
2002	Holland*
2003	Malaysia*
2004	Thailand/Hong Kong*
2008	Spain*
2011	USA*

*Pre-season trip

— MASCOTS —

While Monty and Maggie Magpie have been part of the scene at St James' Park since the 1990s, they are by no means United's first mascots.

The early 1900s were notable for the appearance of a black and white Great Dane dog christened Rex on team photos, while fans travelling by ship to the 1924 FA Cup Final at Wembley were accompanied by a large toy cat named Felix.

A familiar sight at post-WW2 games meanwhile was Peter Anderson – clad in a black and white striped suit, shoes and top hat, with the motto "Howay United" on the back of his jacket, Anderson had a similarly dressed assistant and both appear on Pathe newsreel footage of the 1952/53 season.

A large Magpie dummy appeared at club photo sessions in the early 1980s, whilst an elderly gentleman in a striped suit reprised Anderson's 1950s touchline strolls around that time.

— WEMBLEY MISCELLANY —

A few random facts related to the Toon's numerous Twin Towers trips:

Year	Guest of honour	Referee
1924	HRH The Duke of York	W.E. Russell
1932	King George V	Percy Harper
1951	King George VI	William Ling
1952	Winston Churchill (Prime Minister)	Arthur Ellis
1955	Queen Elizabeth II	Reg Leafe
1974	HRH Princess Anne	Gordon Kew
1976*	Duke of Norfolk	Jack Taylor
1996**	James Ross (Littlewoods Chairman)	Paul Durkin
1998	Duke and Duchess of Kent	Paul Durkin
1999	HRH Prince of Wales	Peter Jones

Note: All the above were FA Cup finals, except for *League Cup Final and **Charity Shield.

Organised community singing first became a fixture at Wembley Finals in 1927, when a TP Radcliff aka 'The Man in White' appeared on a podium to conduct the crowds. Appearing on the first songsheet was 'Abide with Me'. By the time Newcastle made their trio of successful Wembley appearances in the 1950s, the baton has been passed on to Arthur Caiger.

Incidentally, Arthur Ellis, the referee of the 1952 final went on to be better known to many as 'Uncle Arthur', resident judge of the hit TV programme *It's A Knockout!*.

In 1974, when Newcastle played Liverpool at Wembley, TV personality and *Generation Game* host Bruce Forsyth attempted to lead the singing.

The Magpies had the misfortune to oppose the Premier League Champions in both the 1998 and 1999 finals, with victories for Arsenal and Manchester United seeing them complete a domestic double. The Red Devils would then go on to make that a treble, defeating Bayern Munich in the Champions League final just days later, after which Alex Ferguson was knighted.

While Newcastle supporters endured miserable days out at both the 1998 and 1999 finals, for one follower in particular the latter tie was to have far-reaching consequences.

Former Magpie midfielder Lee Clark had moved to Wearside two years earlier and helped the red and whites clinch a return to the top-flight – and the resumption of derby matches – the previous weekend. However his decision to don a t-shirt bearing the slogan "Sad Mackem Bastards" while en route to Wembley with a group of fellow Newcastle fans soon got him into hot water – when a photograph of him began to circulate on the internet and the North East press got wind of it.

Manager Peter Reid failed to see the funny side, however, and the Black Cats swiftly transfer-listed Clark, who subsequently claimed that he'd previously spoken to his boss and expressed a desire to move on. Lee soon got his wish and was transferred to Fulham, managed by Paul Bracewell.

— NEWCASTLE UNITED'S LEAGUE RECORD 1893–2012 —

| SEASON | (DIV) | P | Home | | | | | Away | | | | | Pts | Pos |
			W	D	L	F	A	W	D	L	F	A		
1893/94	2	28	12	1	1	44	10	3	5	6	22	29	36	4th
1894/95	2	30	11	1	3	51	28	1	2	12	21	56	27	10th
1895/96	2	30	14	0	1	57	14	2	2	11	16	36	34	5th
1896/97	2	30	13	1	1	42	13	4	0	11	14	39	35	5th
1897/98	2	30	14	0	1	43	10	7	3	5	21	22	45	2nd (Promoted)
1898/99	1	34	9	3	5	33	18	2	5	10	16	30	30	13th
1899/00	1	34	10	5	2	34	15	3	5	9	19	28	36	5th
1900/01	1	34	10	5	2	27	13	4	5	8	15	24	38	6th
1901/02	1	34	11	3	3	41	14	3	6	8	7	20	37	3rd
1902/03	1	34	12	1	4	31	11	2	3	12	10	40	32	14th
1903/04	1	34	12	3	2	31	13	6	3	8	27	32	42	4th
1904/05	1	34	14	1	2	41	12	9	1	7	31	21	48	1st (Champions)
1905/06	1	38	12	4	3	49	23	6	3	10	25	25	43	4th
1906/07	1	38	18	1	0	51	12	4	6	9	23	34	51	1st (Champions)
1907/08	1	38	11	4	4	41	24	4	8	7	24	30	42	4th
1908/09	1	38	14	1	4	32	20	10	4	5	33	21	53	1st (Champions)
1909/10	1	38	11	3	5	33	22	8	4	7	37	34	45	4th
1910/11	1	38	8	7	4	37	18	7	3	9	24	25	40	8th
1911/12	1	38	10	4	5	37	25	8	4	7	27	25	44	3rd
1912/13	1	38	8	5	6	30	23	5	3	11	17	24	34	14th
1913/14	1	38	9	6	4	27	18	4	5	10	12	30	37	11th
1914/15	1	38	8	4	7	29	23	3	6	10	17	25	32	15th
1915/19						FIRST WORLD WAR								
1919/20	1	42	11	5	5	31	13	6	4	11	13	26	43	8th
1920/21	1	42	14	3	4	43	18	6	7	8	23	27	50	5th
1921/22	1	42	11	5	5	36	19	7	5	9	23	26	46	7th
1922/23	1	42	13	6	2	31	11	5	6	10	14	26	48	4th
1923/24	1	42	13	5	3	40	21	4	5	12	20	33	42	9th
1924/25	1	42	11	6	4	43	18	5	10	6	18	24	48	6th
1925/26	1	42	13	3	5	59	33	3	7	11	25	42	42	10th
1926/27	1	42	19	1	1	64	20	6	5	10	32	38	56	1st (Champions)

Season	Div	P	W	D	L	F	A	W	D	L	F	A	Pts	Pos
1927/28	1	42	9	7	5	49	41	6	6	9	30	40	43	9th
1928/29	1	42	15	2	4	48	29	4	4	13	22	43	44	10th
1929/30	1	42	13	4	4	52	32	2	3	16	19	60	37	19th
1930/31	1	42	9	2	10	41	45	6	4	11	37	42	36	17th
1931/32	1	42	13	5	3	52	31	5	1	15	28	56	42	11th
1932/33	1	42	15	2	4	44	24	7	3	11	27	39	49	5th
1933/34	1	42	6	11	4	42	29	4	3	14	26	48	34	21st
														(Relegated)
1934/35	2	42	14	2	5	55	25	8	2	11	34	43	48	6th
1935/36	2	42	13	5	3	56	27	7	1	13	32	52	46	8th
1936/37	2	42	11	3	7	45	23	11	2	8	35	33	49	4th
1937/38	2	42	12	4	5	38	18	2	4	15	13	40	36	19th
1938/39	2	42	13	3	5	44	21	5	7	9	17	27	46	9th
1939/46						SECOND WORLD WAR									
1946/47	2	42	11	4	6	60	32	8	6	7	35	30	48	5th
1947/48	2	42	18	1	2	46	13	6	7	8	26	28	56	2nd
														(Promoted)
1948/49	1	42	12	5	4	35	29	8	7	6	35	27	52	4th
1949/50	1	42	14	4	3	49	23	5	8	8	28	32	50	5th
1950/51	1	42	10	6	5	36	22	8	7	6	26	31	49	4th
1951/52	1	42	12	4	5	62	28	6	5	10	36	45	45	8th
1952/53	1	42	9	5	7	34	33	5	4	12	25	37	37	16th
1953/54	1	42	9	2	10	43	40	5	8	8	29	37	38	15th
1954/55	1	42	12	5	4	53	27	5	4	12	36	50	43	8th
1955/56	1	42	12	4	5	49	24	5	3	13	36	46	41	11th
1956/57	1	42	10	5	6	43	31	4	3	14	24	56	36	17th
1957/58	1	42	6	4	11	38	42	6	4	11	35	39	32	19th
1958/59	1	42	11	3	7	40	29	6	4	11	40	51	41	11th
1959/60	1	42	10	5	6	42	32	8	3	10	40	46	44	8th
1960/61	1	42	7	7	7	51	49	4	3	14	35	60	32	21st
														(Relegated)
1961/62	2	42	10	5	6	40	27	5	4	12	24	31	39	11th
1962/63	2	42	11	8	2	48	23	7	3	11	31	36	47	7th
1963/64	2	42	14	2	5	49	26	6	3	12	25	43	45	8th
1964/65	2	42	16	4	1	50	16	8	5	8	31	29	57	1st
														(Promoted)
1965/66	1	42	10	5	6	26	20	4	4	13	24	43	37	15th
1966/67	1	42	9	5	7	24	27	3	4	14	15	54	33	20th
1967/68	1	42	12	7	2	38	20	1	8	12	16	47	41	10th
1968/69	1	42	12	7	2	40	20	3	7	11	21	35	44	9th
1969/70	1	42	14	2	5	42	16	3	11	7	15	19	47	7th

1970/71	1	42	9	9	3	27	16	5	4	12	17	30	41	12th
1971/72	1	42	10	6	5	30	18	5	5	11	19	34	41	11th
1972/73	1	42	12	6	3	35	19	4	7	10	25	32	45	9th
1973/74	1	42	9	6	6	28	21	4	6	11	21	27	38	15th
1974/75	1	42	12	4	5	39	23	3	5	13	20	49	39	15th
1975/76	1	42	11	4	6	51	26	4	5	12	20	36	39	15th
1976/77	1	42	14	6	1	40	15	4	7	10	24	34	49	5th
1977/78	1	42	4	6	11	26	37	2	4	15	16	41	22	21st
														(Relegated)
1978/79	2	42	13	3	5	35	24	4	5	12	16	31	42	8th
1979/80	2	42	13	6	2	35	19	2	8	11	18	30	44	9th
1980/81	2	42	11	7	3	22	13	3	7	11	8	32	42	11th
1981/82	2	42	14	4	3	30	14	4	4	13	22	36	62	9th
1982/83	2	42	13	6	2	43	21	5	7	9	32	32	67	5th
1983/84	2	42	16	2	3	51	18	8	6	7	34	35	80	3rd
														(Promoted)
1984/85	1	42	11	4	6	33	26	2	9	10	22	44	52	14th
1985/86	1	42	12	5	4	46	31	5	7	9	21	41	63	11th
1986/87	1	42	10	4	07	33	29	2	7	12	14	36	47	17th
1987/88	1	40	9	6	5	32	23	5	8	7	23	30	56	8th
1988/89	1	38	3	6	10	19	28	4	4	11	13	35	31	20th
														(Relegated)
1989/90	2	46	17	4	2	51	26	5	10	8	29	29	80	3rd
1990/91	2	46	8	10	5	24	22	6	7	10	25	34	59	11th
1991/92	2	46	9	8	6	38	30	4	5	14	28	54	52	20th
1992/93	(1)	46	16	6	1	58	15	13	3	7	34	23	96	1st
														(Promoted)
1993/94	Pr	42	14	4	3	51	14	9	4	8	31	27	77	3rd
1994/95	Pr	42	14	6	1	46	20	6	6	9	21	27	72	6th
1995/96	Pr	38	17	1	1	38	9	7	5	7	28	28	78	2nd
1996/97	Pr	38	13	3	3	54	20	6	8	5	19	20	68	2nd
1997/98	Pr	38	8	5	6	22	20	3	6	10	13	24	44	13th
1998/99	Pr	38	7	6	6	26	25	4	7	8	22	29	46	13th
1999/00	Pr	38	10	5	4	42	20	4	5	10	21	34	52	11th
2000/01	Pr	38	10	4	5	26	17	4	5	10	18	33	51	11th
2001/02	Pr	38	12	3	4	40	23	9	5	5	34	29	71	4th
2002/03	Pr	38	15	2	2	36	17	6	4	9	27	31	69	3rd
2003/04	Pr	38	11	5	3	33	14	2	12	5	19	26	56	5th
2004/05	Pr	38	7	7	5	25	25	3	7	9	22	32	44	14th
2005/06	Pr	38	11	5	3	28	15	6	2	11	19	27	58	7th
2006/07	Pr	38	7	7	5	23	20	4	3	12	15	27	43	13th

Season	Div	P	W	D	L	F	A	W	D	L	F	A	Pts	Pos
2007/08	Pr	38	8	5	6	25	26	3	5	11	29	39	43	12th
2008/09	Pr	38	5	7	7	24	29	2	6	11	16	30	34	18th
														(Relegated)
2009/10	Ch	46	18	5	0	56	13	12	7	4	34	22	102	1st
														(Promoted)
2010/11	Pr	38	6	8	5	41	27	5	5	9	15	30	46	12th
2011/12	Pr	38	11	5	3	29	17	8	3	8	27	34	65	5th